DELICIOUS

Iceland

Chef Völundur Snær Völundarson

**Delicious Iceland**

Text copyright © Völundur Snær Völundarson and SALKA,
based on original copyrighted material by
Völundur Snær Völundarson and Haukur Ágústsson
in *Delicious Iceland, Tales of unique northern delicacies*

Editor: Darren Foreman

Photographs copyright © Hreinn Hreinsson

Copyright © 2007 SALKA Publisher – Reykjavík – Iceland
www.salkaforlag.is

ISBN 978-9979-768-95-1

Design and layout: Ivan Burkni
Printed in Prentmet ehf.

All rights reserved. No part of this book may be reprinted or reproduced or utilized in any
form or by any electronic, mechanical, or other means, now known or hereafter invented,
including photocopying and recording, or in any information storage or retrieval system,
without permission in writing from the publishers and authors.

Salka

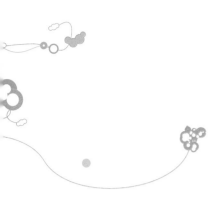

# A Dedication

It is always a source of great pleasure to me when I witness the success of Icelanders who reside and work on foreign soil, such as Chef Völundur Snær Völundarson, who runs one of the finest restaurants in the Bahamas.

Völundur Snær Völundarson not only has made a name for himself in his chosen field, but has also been very active in acquainting people outside Iceland with Icelandic food products and Icelandic culture and history. This cookbook bears ample witness to this.

I have always been fascinated by the many food traditions in the different countries of the world. Food is an important part of every nation's culture and that's especially true in Iceland. Therefore it is with pleasure that I wish Chef Völundur Snær Völundarson every success in his work and hope that he will continue to have the joy and enthusiasm that's apparent in this wonderful book.

*Vigdís Finnbogadóttir*

# We are from Iceland!

I was raised in the countryside of Iceland, a remote island in the northern Atlantic bordering on the Arctic Circle, in a house that sits practically on the banks of one the country's best salmon-fishing rivers. My father, whose parents had farmed that land, worked as a guide on the river and taught me fly-fishing as a boy. My mother, a fantastic cook, taught cooking classes at a school of domestic sciences.

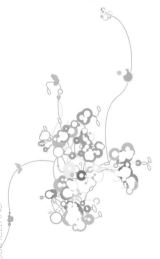

Interest in culinary matters is quite great in my family, but I had no idea I'd become a chef until the age of sixteen, when I was enrolled in athletics at a local college. It was in a required cooking class that the instructor noticed my ability and took me aside. "Worly," he said, "you're on the wrong shelf; you belong on the shelf with the chefs."

This was a turning point in my life. I decided to pursue a career in cooking and entered an apprentice program at The Pearl, one of Reykjavík's finest restaurants. A year later I enrolled in the Icelandic School of Culinary Sciences, from which I received my chef's certificate.

After graduating, I did some cooking in local restaurants, but soon realized that if I wanted to gain valuable culinary experience I'd have to go abroad. I chose France for two reasons: Firstly, I'd always been a great fan of French cuisine; and secondly, I'd studied M. Phillipe Girardon's authoritative book on the subject. In fact, I was fortunate enough to get a place at a Michelin star restaurant run by Chef Girardon himself.

After France, I travelled to the United States, working first as a temporary chef in Oregon and later as a chef de partie at the famous Charlie Trotter's Restaurant in Chicago, the latter undoubtedly being my greatest learning experience. With cookbooks being written and a tv series being produced, as well as the day to day service in the restaurant, it was an adventurous time.

**But** it was there that the idea to write my own cookbook first took form in my mind. Chef Trotter frequently sent me into the dining room to tell the guests about the native food of my country and as I described these unique ingredients and recipes I realized that Icelandic cuisine and its fine produce, fish, and meat were almost a well-kept secret. As my pride in my country and culture increased, so did my longing to introduce this food to the world.

I realized, though, that completing the project I had in mind would take the cooperation of a dedicated and close-knit team. For the book's illustrations, I had only one choice in mind. Hreinn Hreinsson is not only one of Iceland's most renowned photographers, he's also one of my closest friends. He comes from the northern part of the country, like me, and shares a deep love of its landscape and wildlife. Most importantly, he's an artist whose work has been seen all over the world. It takes only one look at the photos within to realize that if there is any merit in this book, I share it with Hreinn.

# Finding someone to assist me with writing the text was another, quite difficult matter. But after consulting with my father, whose sound judgement is something I've relied on in the past, I contacted Mr. Haukur Ágústsson, a former clergyman and one-time college principal. Though he was essentially retired and working on a project of his own, I managed to convince him and soon he and his wife joined me in Grand Bahama to work on the project. His contribution to the book has been invaluable and I whole-heartedly thank him.

In addition to my two main partners there are many others who have assisted in putting this book together. There's not enough space to name them all, but one I'd like to mention has been a constant sourse of inspiration to me: my co-worker in many of the cooking sessions, and good friend, chef Gunnar Chan.

I really feel I've been lucky to find the dedicated and gifted collaborators who've helped with this book. They've been encouraging, helpful, and inspiring. I'm extremely proud of their work and thankful to them for helping me make my dream come true. As a matter of fact, as the work progressed the dream was no longer mine alone, but became a collective one, shared by all of us.

**I now** share it with you, dear reader; and hope that you, too, will appreciate this beautiful country and its food products, as well as my approach to Icelandic cuisine.

Chef Völundur Snær Völundarson

# BENEATH THE WAVES

# River Salmon

Iceland is, of course, well known for its fishing. For centuries we've relied on it for both sustenance and income. But although Icelandic trawlers haul in great amounts from the neighbouring seas, it's the local fishing, in the lakes and rivers, that most appeals to me. And I've been fortunate to have spent a great deal of time at two of Iceland's most renowned fishing areas.

I was brought up on the banks of the Laxá, one of the more famous salmon-fishing rivers in Iceland. It was there, under the guidance of my father, that I learned to appreciate both the river and the noble sport of fly fishing. But I'm also indebted to the many fine salmon fishermen, Icelandic and foreign, who every summer came to fish and to enjoy the exquisite beauty of the river and its fascinating surroundings, and from whom I learned a great deal.

Salmon rivers are numerous in Iceland. In older times it was customary for farmers having access to salmon rivers to drag them with nets. In many cases the catch was immense and what fish could not be consumed fresh was salted or smoked and the roes, if they could not be used fresh, were used for bread or in soups. Still, preserving the great number of fish caught was an almost insurmountable problem. Salmon was such a frequent fare on some farms that quite often farmhands, hired by salmon fishing farmers, stipulated in their contracts how often salmon was to be served to them during the week.

But I've come to cherish the fine taste and texture of river salmon. My mother often had it on the table, where it was always greeted enthusiastically. In my work as a chef I use many different methods to prepare salmon, but I have to admit that nothing really beats salmon cooked the way my mother did, served with melted butter and freshly harvested potatoes.

Preheat the oven to 225° F / 110°C. Place the carrots, onion, celery, and chervil stems on a baking tray and bake in the oven for 20 minutes. Next, season the salmon with salt and pepper and rub 1 tablespoon of olive oil into the flesh. Place the seasoned salmon on top of the vegetables and bake for 15-20 minutes at 200° F / 95°C. Remove the tray from the oven and reserve until ready to assemble on the plate.

Using the potato slice to weigh down the skin and keep it flat while cooking, place a piece of salmon skin in a non-stick pan over low heat. Once it starts to brown, turn it over and complete the crisping process. Repeat this for the other three pieces of skin. Reserve the skins in a warm, dry place.

In a medium-size pot, combine the cauliflower and milk. Bring to a simmer and cook covered for 30 minutes or until soft. Remove from the heat and, still covered, allow to cool. Once cool, place in a blender and mix until a fine silky purée is formed. Add 3 tablespoons of olive oil and purée again. Season with salt and pepper.

Cut the blanched Brussels sprouts into quarters, lengthwise. In a sauté pan on medium heat, add the quartered Brussels sprouts and 2 tablespoons of olive oil. Cook until golden brown and season with salt and pepper

Spoon the cauliflower purée onto the middle of the plate. Place the salmon directly on top of the cauliflower purée. Place the browned Brussels sprouts around the salmon and spoon the Sauvignon Blanc froth over the fish and around the plate. Place the crispy salmon skin on top and garnish with the chervil sprigs.

# SLOW-ROASTED SALMON
## with Cauliflower Purée and Sauvignon Blanc Froth

**(serves four)**

1 carrot, peeled and cut into strips
1 celery stalk, peeled and cut into strips
1 onion, peeled and sliced
4 sprigs chervil, reserving the stems
4 3-oz portions of salmon, skin removed and reserved
Salt and pepper
6 tablespoons olive oil
One slice of potato, app. 4 inches long and 1 inch thick
1 cup cauliflower florets
½ cup milk
12 Brussels sprouts, scored on the bottom
and blanched (see appendix)
Sauvignon Blanc froth (see appendix)

**I learned** these gravlax recipes while working with my parents at the salmon fisherman's lodge on the river Laxá in the summer of 1991 and have used no others since. They've been a family secret, but I've been given permission to reveal them for the first time.

## The Curing Mixture

11 oz salt
13 oz sugar
½ tablespoon ground white pepper
4 tablespoons lemon pepper
4 tablespoons fennel powder
½ cup dry dill

# MY FATHER'S
# GRAVLAX RECIPE
## with My Mother's Exquisite
## Dill and Mustard Sauce

(serves four)

Mix the ingredients, except the dill, together thoroughly. Fillet the salmon, but don't skin it.

In a deep tray, arrange the salmon meat in several layers, skin side down, with a liberal spreading of the prepared curing mixture in between each layer. Cover tightly with plastic wrap and refrigerate for 36 hours. When the time is up, turn the fillets over, rewrap the tray, and return to the refrigerator for another 36 hours.

**Finish the process** by scraping off the excess curing mixture and cutting the fillets into slices appropriate for each use. Meat not immediately used should be refrigerated or frozen.

## The Gravlax Sauce

6.8 oz sweet mustard
1.7 oz Dijon mustard
1.7 oz dry dill
1.7 oz honey
6.8 oz vegetable oil
3.4 oz mayonnaise
A dash of Cognac (if desired)

Mix the ingredients together thoroughly, adding the oil last. A dash of Cognac may be stirred in if desired.

Serve the gravlax with slices of toast and a liberal amount of sauce.

# SALMON
## with Blini Cakes, Horseradish Cream and Trout Roe

**(serves four)**

½ a fillet of smoked salmon, thick portion
Segments of one lemon
1 bunch arugula salad
½ red onion, finely diced
3 oz trout roe
3 oz capers
Dill, for decoration
Blini (see appendix)
Horseradish cream (see appendix)

**Put a cake** of blini in the centre of a plate and spread a good amount of horseradish cream on top of the cake. Arrange some segments of the lemon on the layer of cream, along with a bunch of the arugula salad and a liberal amount of diced red onions and capers. On top of this put a slice of the smoked salmon and then finish the arrangement off with a nice dab of horseradish cream topped with a heaping teaspoon of trout roes. Finally, decorate the dish by scattering a sprig of dill over it.

This dish is a very savoury one, offering the fragrance and taste of the smoked salmon, mingled pleasantly with the sourness of lemon and the distinctive flavor of the horseradish cream.

# Lake char

Mývatn (Midge Lake) is one the most popular places of interest in Iceland, being visited by tens of thousands every year. It's far inland in the north-eastern part of the country and is an equally great attraction to the geologist, the birdwatcher, and the tourist.

**The inhabitants** of the Mývatn area are proud and resourceful people, intensely fond of their bit of Iceland. For the most part they're farmers or fisherman, depending for their livelihood on the raising of sheep and on fishing for trout, especially char, in the lake.

**Though fishing** is done in the summer, I find the winter fishing to be the most fun. The fishermen drive out on the lake in their cars or on snowmobiles, racing across the smooth ice and leaving great clouds of snow in their wakes. They drill holes and put nets down, pulling them out from under the ice using a special, hand-operated apparatus. It's a fascinating and beautiful sight, with the green-hued water at the bottom and the char accumulating on the ice near the hole.

The catch of char from Mývatn can be quite great and is very much sought after by people exacting in their choice of smoked trout. This is understandable, since it has a special, savoury flavour coming from the rich stock of midges and midge larvae it feeds on. No less important, though, is the method of smoking the char, which is done by local fisherman and is based on an old and time-tested tradition. The char is imbued with a pleasant and strong aroma and a taste that is exceptionally full and satisfying.

My many experiences at Mývatn make it a very special place to me and I'll certainly continue to visit the area for the rest of my life. Each time the opportunity has arisen I find myself filled with anticipation and eagerness, for to my mind it's one of the most marvellous and enchanting places on the planet.

10.5 oz smoked char
24 baby asparagus, blanched (see appendix)
1 tablespoon extra virgin olive oil
½ pint fish stock (see appendix)
12 oz skinned cod fillets
½ oz gelatin powder
Juice from one lemon
½ pint whipping cream, whipped
Salt
White pepper

# SMOKED CHAR
## and Cod Mousse Roll with Asparagus
### (serves four)

Bring the fish stock to a boil and then reduce to a simmer. Add the cod and gently poach for ten minutes. Remove and allow to cool.

In a saucepan, melt the gelatin powder completely with two to three tablespoons of the hot fish stock, then stir into the rest of the stock and set aside to cool. When it has cooled, place the stock in the refrigerator until it becomes "oily" and starts to set.

Put the cod in a food processor and blend finely, adding one-fourth of a cup of fish stock and then the lemon juice. Next, run the blended cod through a fine-meshed sieve using a stiff spatula, making the mixture very fine and smooth. Into this, gently mix in the chilled fish stock and then fold in the whipped cream. Season with salt and pepper.

Wipe a counter top with a clean, damp cloth and place a twelve by twelve inch sheet of plastic wrap on the dampened area. Cut the smoked char fillet into thin slices, preferably along the length of the fillet, and arrange them side by side and slightly overlapping on top of the plastic wrap, covering an area ten inches long and eight inches wide. Next, using a long spatula, spread an even layer of the cod mousse, one-fourth of an inch thick, on top of the layer of char, leaving half an inch of the char uncovered at the far edge. Starting from the near edge of the plastic wrap, roll up the cod and char, being careful not to roll the plastic wrap into the food. Close the roll using the uncovered edge of the smoked char. Finally, wrap the roll tightly with the plastic wrap and place it in the refrigerator to cool and set.

To finish, toss the asparagus in some oil and season with salt and pepper. Then arrange the stalks side by side in the center of a plate. Cut a three-quarter inch thick slice of the fish roll and place it on the bed of asparagus.

# Halibut

Halibut has always been a great favourite with Icelanders. In the old days it was considered practically holy, as is evidenced by one of the Icelandic names for it, which is "heilagfiski" or holy fish. Various tales were told about the halibut, some of them mythical, but others showing knowledge of the habits of this noble fish, such as the one relating that during the sea-bird egging season, the halibut flock to the feet of the cliffs to eat the eggs that are kicked off ledges and fall into the sea.

Freshly caught halibut was eaten boiled or fried with potatoes and thought to be food fit for kings. If the halibut was to be smoked or dried it was halved lengthwise all the way down to the tail and then flung over rims suspended by the tail end. For better curing the sides of the fish were cut in strips similar to a comb and the strips held apart with small sticks of wood to ensure that the air or smoke had good access to the fish. In some places smoked halibut was eaten raw, whereas the dried one always was. Another method for preserving halibut was salting it in brine. The salted fish had to be de-salted in fresh water before cooking and was eaten boiled with, for example, melted butter and potatoes.

# HALIBUT
# CARPACCIO
## with Brunoise and Sizzling Hot Sesame Seed Oil

**(serves four)**

10 oz halibut fillet
½ cup brunoise (see appendix)
½ cup sesame seed oil
2 tablespoons black sesame seeds, toasted

Sushi can be prepared a number of ways; here's one a bit out of the ordinary, but definitely worth a try.

Cut the halibut fillet into strips about one eighth of an inch in thickness, three to four inches in length, and an inch in width. Arrange the strips side by side on a plate, forming a flat square about five to six inches in length. Scatter the brunoise quite liberally on the halibut square.

Heat the oil until it's very hot and then pour it over the halibut and brunoise. It should sizzle as it hits the arrangement. The hot oil seals the fillet strips, heating them somewhat, while the inside of the fish remains moist and raw. This process offers a tantalyzing contrast between the cooked and raw fish, the crispness of the vegetables, and the added tingle of the sizzling hot oil.

3 cups olive oil
1 lemon, quartered
4 basil leaf stems
2 teaspoon fennel seed
4 3-oz portions of halibut, skin and bones removed
2 tablespoons olive oil
12 pitted Kalamata olives, sliced in 6 pieces
2 tomatoes, skinned, deseeded, and finely diced
2 teaspoons lemon juice
16 tiny basil leaves
Salt and pepper
Zest of one lemon, finely julienned
Lemon scented potato purée (see appendix)

# OLIVE OIL-POACHED HALIBUT

## with Lemon Scented Potato Purée and Kalamata Olive-Tomato Vinaigrette

(serves four)

I love halibut, especially when you can get the larger fish from very cold waters. The rich cooking method of poaching in olive oil goes well with the delicate texture of the fish. Tomatoes and olives are readily available in the warmer months, the basil adds a Mediterranean feel to our local products, and the acidity of the lemon balances well with the creamy potato purée.

In a medium sauce pot, place the olive oil, lemon, basil stems, and 1 teaspoon of fennel seed. On very low heat bring the temperature of the oil to 150° F/65°C. Next, place the halibut in the oil, nestling it on top of the basil stems for support. Cook for 12-15 minutes until the flesh is starting to take on a white, opaque colour. Remove the pan from the heat and let rest. Once the oil is slightly cooler remove the halibut and season with salt and pepper.

In a small sauce pan on medium heat toast the remaining fennel seed until you can smell the aroma of the seeds. Next, add 2 tablespoons of olive oil. Once the seeds are coated in oil, add the sliced olives, tomatoes, and lemon juice. Swirl the pan until the lemon juice and olive oil are emulsified. Season with salt and pepper and at the last minute add the small basil leaves.

Place one nice dollop of lemon scented potato purée in the middle of the plate. Rest the halibut directly on top of the purée. Next, spoon the vinaigrette over the fish and let the juices drip down over it.

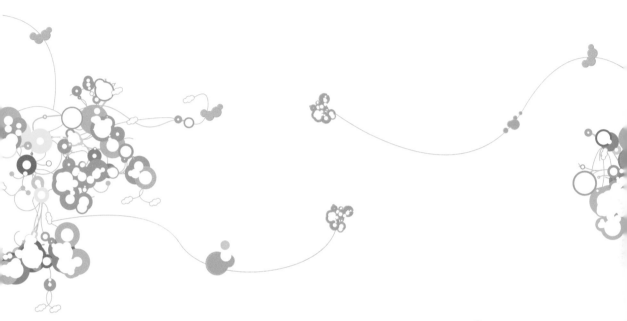

# Herring

I've always found it quite astounding, since herring is so abundant in Icelandic waters, that the early Icelanders rarely used it for food. As a matter of fact it was considered practically inedible and, though sometimes eaten smoked or in fish balls, was mainly used for bait.

**But around** the turn of the twentieth century a herring rush was on and a great many seaside villages sprung up around herring-salting stations and fish meal factories. Today the rush is over and, though Icelanders eat more now than in former times, herring is mainly processed, salted or pickled for export.

# SILVER OF THE SEA
## with Potato Salad
(serves four)

4 plain-pickled herring fillets
½ red onion, sliced
12 small red potatoes
Dill, whole and chopped
4 tablespoons olive oil
1 bunch watercress
1 teaspoon lemon juice
Salt and pepper

In Iceland herring is called the "Silver of the Sea." Although its scales are certainly silvery, it most likely acquired this name because herring was the source of great wealth during the first half of the twentieth century.

The herring processed for consumption is for the most part either salted or pickled. The pickled variety is a great delicacy and is frequently used for starters in a kind of salad.

Begin by cutting the pickled herring fillets into pieces about an inch in length and finely slicing the red onion. Put these aside while the salad is being prepared.

Boil the potatoes, allow them to cool, and then halve them. Chop the watercress and some of the dill and mix together with the potatoes, the oil and lemon juice. Season to taste with salt and pepper.

Arrange the potato mixture in small bowls or plates, top with the onion slices, and crown with the pieces from one fillet of pickled herring. Garnish with whole dill.

This comparatively simple course makes a savory and surprising starter.

# Eel

Eel is a most peculiar type of fish. It travels the distance from its spawning areas off the coasts of Bermuda and then follows the currents of the Gulf Stream to the shores of Europe and even to far off Iceland. This trip takes about three years.

**Icelanders** didn't eat eel much in the old days, but views have changed quite a lot since then as far as food and things edible are concerned. Now eel is considered a delicacy in my home country and is fished quite a bit, for the most part in the wetlands in the south, but also a bit elsewhere in the country.

As a matter of fact, in the summer of 1998, in my home county of Aðaldalur (Main Valley) in the north, I was fortunate enough to experience the thrill and excitement of eel fishing. It was summer, with fine weather and the midnight sun hovering on the horizon, so the short trip to the wetlands where we intended to trap the eel was very pleasant indeed. My companions were knowledgeable about the most likely places for eel, so I had little to do but enjoy the trip and take as lively a part in the proceedings as I possibly could.

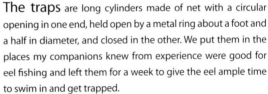

**The traps** are long cylinders made of net with a circular opening in one end, held open by a metal ring about a foot and a half in diameter, and closed in the other. We put them in the places my companions knew from experience were good for eel fishing and left them for a week to give the eel ample time to swim in and get trapped.

On returning to the wetlands, we took out the traps and found that, indeed, some eels had swum in and not managed to find their way out again. They writhed fiercely and were rather hard to get hold of, since the skin is exceedingly smooth and slippery, but we were determined not to let our catch get away. So after some fighting with the wily things we managed to transfer them into old milk cans holding some water, into which we scattered a liberal amount of salt to numb the eel and make it less slippery. This worked all right and soon we were on our way home with our catch ready to be processed through salting and smoking.

12 oz fillets of smoked eel
Pinch of micro basil
Edamame mousse (see appendix)
Sesame seed sauce (see appendix)
Wasabi oil (see appendix)
Pickled red onion (see appendix)
1 small mango, diced

# SMOKED EEL
## with Edamame Mousse, Sesame Seed Sauce and Wasabi Oil

(serves four)

When removing the smoked eel from the package take care not to smash or tear the meat. Place it on a flat surface with the skin side down and make an incision close to the tail, barely penetrating the skin. Now flip the eel over and, starting at the incision, gently pull the skin from the meat, keeping it firmly on the board section by section to prevent breakage. Once the skin has been removed, cut the eel in half lengthwise and then into diamond-shaped pieces about two inches in length.

Begin by slightly heating the eel in a broiler. On a bed of edamame mousse, alternate layers of pickled onion and diced mango with layers of the eel. Drizzle the wasabi oil and sesame seed sauce around the arrangement and top with a sprig of micro basil.

This dish is satisfying to both the taste buds and the eyes. The eel has a strong, smokey taste emphasized by the wasabi oil, while its dark brown colour stands in delicious contrast to the edamame paste.

# Capelin

In wintertime these small, silvery fish abound in the sea around Iceland, where they move about in huge schools.

Capelin was not fished much by the Icelanders of old, but it frequently happened, when heavy winds drove the waves roaring against the coastline, that large amounts of capelin were heaped up on the black sand beaches.

## Fish liver

The liver of many species of fish was quite popular as food in Iceland in the old days, but today the most sought after is the liver of cod. Though small quantities are eaten as is, the majority of cod livers are melted down for the production of cod liver oil, which is either exported or sold locally as health food.

Many believe that the consumption of fish oil played a vital role in getting my ancestors through the harsh periods in my nation's history. Certainly, scientific data backs up the healthful benefits of cod liver oil and I know many people who believe that starting each day with it keeps them healthy, vigorous, and going.

# Shellfish

In the old days shellfish weren´t eaten much in Iceland, although mussels, scallops, Iceland cyprines, sea urchin and various conchs abound in Icelandic waters. The same is true of shrimp and lobster, which were also underutilized. The only type of shellfish that was consumed at all was blue mussel and this only in rare instances.

In more recent times, however, scallop, sea urchin, shrimp and lobster have been extensively scooped up for processing and small-scale blue mussel farming has been started in a few places. This development is a very positive one, since the sea around Iceland is exceptionally free from pollution and thus well-suited for sea farming of various kinds.

4 large scallops
Bunch of rosemary
Bunch of thyme
Bunch of coconut flakes
1 cup Absolut Citron Vodka
½ cup water
¼ oz gelatin
Scallion marmalade (see appendix)
1 oz Osetra caviar
Pickling liquid (see appendix)
Some strands of Majenta lace
4 lime segments
Lemon oil (see appendix)
Salt and pepper

# COLD-SMOKED
# SCALLOP
## with Vodka Jelly, Scallion
## Marmalade and Osetra Caviar

(serves four)

Put the scallops in the pickling liquid and marinate for half an hour. When this step is over fill a deep pan with ice, close it with a sheet of aluminum foil, and put it on a grill. Throw some rosemary, thyme and coconut flakes on top of the embers for smoke flavor, then put the scallops on top of the foil and shut the grill lid. The ice in the pan keeps the scallops cool, so they are in fact "cold-smoked." After smoking for twenty minutes, turn the scallops and smoke twenty minutes more.

To prepare the vodka jelly, heat half a cup of water in a pot, dissolve the gelatin in it, and add the vodka. Allow the jelly to cool until firm, then chop it into small cubes about a quarter of an inch in size.

When this course is served, the cubes of vodka jelly are used to make a bed in the center of a plate. Onto the bed we put one piece of lime segment and some Majenta lace. The bed should be large enough for the jelly to reach well beyond the scallop, which is put on top. The jelly should resemble crunched ice, giving an image of icy freshness. On top of the scallop we put a layer of scallion marmalade, and then a generous scoop of caviar, the whole resembling a miniature mountain with a slide of caviar coming down the slope. Drizzle some lemon oil around the arrangement for decoration and flavor.

# CITRUS
# SHRIMP SALAD
## with Sesame Seed Oil

**(serves four)**

12 oz shrimp
½ onion
½ avocado
1 blood orange, segmented and diced
1 grape fruit, segmented and diced
1 tablespoon chives, chopped
1 ½ tablespoons quality sesame seed oil
Pinches of red orach for garnish

Chop the onion, avocado, blood orange, and grapefruit segments into small cubes. Mix thoroughly with the shrimp, sesame seed oil, and chives, taking care not to crush the avocado, which tends to be delicate. Season with salt and pepper and garnish with a pinch of red orach on top.

This is a great starter dish, fresh and full-flavored. I think it's ideal served in smaller vessels, such as Chinese porcelain spoons.

24 mussels
3 oz butter
2 cups white wine
1 stem lemon grass
½ red onion, diced
Juice from two lemons
1 clove garlic, crushed
1 tablespoon grape seed oil
2 tablespoons chopped chives
Salt and pepper

# WHITE WINE-
# STEAMED MUSSELS
## in Herb and Lemon Grass Sauce
**(serves four)**

Begin by cutting the lemon grass in half and beating it with a meat mallet to release the flavor. Then put the lemon grass, onions, and a bit of garlic into a pot and sautée in grape seed oil. Add the mussels, squeeze some lemon juice over them, add the chives, and finally the white wine. Cover the pot and turn up the heat, steaming the mussels until they open. At that time, remove the mussels from the pot and take off one half of each shell, so that the meat remains on the half-shell.

Next, remove the lemon grass from the broth, add the butter and stir until it has completely melted. Season with salt and pepper.

Arrange the shells in a long, narrow dish, six for each serving, and pour a little sauce into each one. French baguettes make an excellent accompaniment, as they can be used to soak up the extra sauce.

16 whole Iceland Cyprines
2 roma tomatoes, finely diced
¾ cup white beans, cooked (see appendix)

**Champagne Sabayon**
3 egg yolks
2 teaspoons minced shallots
¼ teaspoon salt
⅓ cup champagne
⅛ teaspoon freshly ground black pepper

# GRATINATED CYPRINES
## with White Beans, Tomatoes and Champagne Sabayon
**(serves four)**

Although shellfish abound along the Icelandic coastline, where they thrive beautifully in the cold, semi-arctic waters, it wasn't until recently that inhabitants of the country discovered this delicious food. Nowadays there's quite a demand for it and even a budding industry in the farming of shellfish for both inland consumption and export.

For the Champagne Sabayon combine all the ingredients in a small, stainless-steel bowl. Set the bowl over a pot of simmering water and whisk for about 3 minutes, until the sabayon begins to thicken.

Open the Iceland Cyprines using a dinner knife. Loosen the fish gently from the shell and place the shell with the fish in it on a baking sheet. Put the cooked beans and the diced tomatoes into each shell and season with salt and pepper.

Put the baking sheet with the shells under a broiler for about 2 minutes. Then put about a tablespoon of the sabayon sauce on top of each shell and broil for another minute or until the food is golden brown. Finally, take the baking sheet and the shells out of the broiler and this dish is ready. Serve warm.

# HARÐFISKUR (Hard Fish)

There are several types of food specific to Iceland that I'm especially fond of and harðfiskur (Hard Fish) is definitely one of them. I greatly prefer it to other snack foods and if given the chance and supply enough can nibble at it almost incessantly.

**In the** old days, before the introduction of affordable salt, processing fish as "harðfiskur" was the only way to preserve it for shipment to the farmers living far from the fishing stations, who ate it throughout the year. The fish, usually cod, was split open and hung up in lath-walled sheds until it was bone-dry and hard, in which state it could be stored for long periods. However, the fish was too solid to be eaten. So, in order to make it more fit for consumption, it was placed on a large stone and beaten with a stone hammer until it became flaky. The fish was then torn apart and eaten with fat, such as butter, drippings or a whipped mixture of liver oil and tallow.

**Harðfiskur** was stable food in Iceland in the old days. Also, as fishing progressed in the country, it came to be one of the most important export products, being carried in whole shiploads to various ports in Europe, and later, to countries throughout Africa.

Akin to hard fish is hung fish. This is treated nearly the same way as hard fish, though the process is stopped when the fish has reached a semi-hard stage. It's then firm to the touch and has a strong, fresh smell. This food is always eaten cooked with, for example, tallow fritters and potatoes and is considered by many to be a great delicacy.

## OATMEAL-CRUSTED
# FILLET OF PLAICE
### with Spring Salad and Cold Caraway and Cucumber Sauce

**(serves four)**

### The Plaice

1.7 lb fillet of plaice

2 eggs

1 cup milk

1 ½ cups oatmeal

1 tablespoon roasted caraway seeds

1 cucumber

1 cup sour cream

Juice from two lemons

½ cup grape seed oil

3.5 oz butter

Salt and pepper

### For the Salad

Lemon vinaigrette **(see appendix)**

2 oz cutting celery

2 oz purple kohlrabi

2 oz watercress

Trim the plaice fillet and cut into pieces about two inches across. Beat the eggs and milk to make an egg wash and place the fish in the liquid. Spread a liberal amount of oatmeal on a plate and season with salt and pepper. Remove the fish from the egg wash and roll in the oatmeal until it's completely covered.

Put the grape seed oil and a little butter in a medium-hot pan and sautée the plaice until the coating is light brown and crispy, about two minutes on each side.

Roast the caraway seeds in a dry pan and then grind finely. Peel the cucumber, halve lengthwise, and scrape out the seeds. In a blender, thoroughly mix the cucumber with, first, the caraway seeds, then the lemon juice, and finally the sour cream. When the sauce is finished, season with salt and pepper.

For the salad, remove the ends of the watercress and toss the remainder, along with the celery and kohlrabi, with the lemon vinaigrette.

Using some of the sauce, make a pool in the middle of each plate and put some salad on top to form a bed. Stack the plaice fillets on the salad.

# MOTHER'S PAN-SAUTEED HADDOCK

## with Mashed Potatoes

### (serves four)

This course is dedicated to an excellent cook: my mother, Halla Loftsdóttir. It may seem too simple to be included in a cookbook, but I can assure you that it's really splendid. And when you think about it, where, really, is most of the world's cooking done, but in mother's kitchen, where she consistently works her wondrous magic?

Trim the skinned fillet of haddock and cut it into pieces about two to three inches in width. Roll the pieces in flour seasoned with some salt and pepper, immerse in beaten eggs and finally coat the fillet pieces thoroughly with bread crumbs. Sauté the prepared pieces of fillet in butter in a medium-hot pan until they are golden brown and the bread crumb crust has become somewhat crispy. Sauté the slices of red onion in the pan along with the fillets.

Cut the lime in half, dip it in sugar and sauté it in butter in a separate pan (cut side down) until the sugar has caramelized.

Boil the potatoes in water until they're soft. Drain the water off and mash the potatoes in the pot with a potato masher, adding the cream and butter. Keep the pot on low heat to melt the butter. Mix thoroughly until the potatoes are completely smooth, then season to taste with salt and pepper.

To serve, arrange a bed of mashed potatoes on a plate, and place the fillet of haddock on top. Rest the caramelized lime on the fillet. (Its juice is to be squeezed on the fillet when it's eaten.) Ladle some of the butter and sautéed onions from the sauté pan onto the arrangement, keeping some on the side along with extra mashed potatoes.

There you have it: my mother's recipe. The only thing I've added is the caramelized half of lime.

### The Haddock

1.5 lb fillet of haddock, skinned
1 red onion, sliced
4 oz butter
½ cup flour
2 eggs
1 cup bread crumbs
2 limes
2 tablespoons sugar
Salt and pepper

### The Mashed Potatoes

1 lb peeled potatoes
½ cup cream
2 oz butter
Salt and pepper

8 Squid
4 Roma tomatoes
Bunches of rosemary
Bunches of thyme
Bunches of birch bark
1 tablespoon grape seed oil
Portobello mushroom risotto (see appendix)
Pinches of micro bok choy
3 oz butter

# SAUTÉED
# STUFFED SQUID
## with Portobello Mushroom Risotto, Squid Tentacles and Smoked Roma Tomato Sauce

(serves four)

Small squid is used for this course, both the body and tentacles. Begin by removing the tentacles and the innards, taking care not to rupture the ink bladder. Clean both the body and the tentacles. Then, stuff the squid body with the Portobello mushroom risotto, taking care not to overstuff. Close the open end with a toothpick and sauté the stuffed squid bodies in butter until golden brown. Do not overcook the squid, or it will become chewy. After sautéing, remove the toothpicks.

Next, sauté the tentacles in grape seed oil, add strips of squid and season with salt and white pepper, adding some butter toward the end. Sauté the tentacles and strips of squid until they start curling up a bit.

For the sauce, start by throwing some rosemary, thyme and birch bark on the embers in a grill. Put the tomatoes on the rack, and close the lid completely to keep the smoke inside. The tomatoes are left to cure in the smoke for an hour or so. When the tomatoes are done, peel their skin off and churn them into sauce in a mixer. Heat the sauce close to the boiling point and season to taste with salt, pepper and fresh lime juice. Finally, whip cubes of cold butter vigorously into the sauce with a hand blender until the sauce becomes somewhat frothy.

When this dish is served, the frothy smoked-tomato sauce is used to make a pool in the center of a plate. The sautéed squid is arranged in the center of the sauce and the arrangement decorated with some micro bok choy and the curled strips of squid.

# SAUTÉED
# TURBOT FILLETS
## with Baked Cherry Tomatoes, Micro Broccoli Sprouts and Beurre Blanc Sauce

(serves four)

1.5 lb turbot fillets
16 cherry tomatoes, blanched (see appendix)
Beurre blanc sauce (see appendix)
4 oz micro broccoli sprouts
Lemon vinaigrette (see appendix)
Salt and pepper

Trim the turbot fillets, if needed, and cut them into pieces about two to three inches in width. Season with salt and pepper. Sauté the fillets in butter until golden brown.

Cut a small cross in the end of each tomato and blanch them in boiling water. Remove them and peel off the skin. Season with salt and pepper and bake for five minutes in an oven preheated to 350°F/175°C.

Arrange four of the tomatoes on a plate, rest the sautéed fillet of turbo on top, and pour some beurre blanc sauce around it all for flavor and decoration. Toss the micro broccoli sprouts in lemon vinaigrette and add them to the arrangement for freshness and further enhancement.

# MONKFISH
## with Seaweed Salad and Wasabi Capelin Roes
### (serves four)

6 oz monkfish, blanched (see appendix)
2 oz seaweed salad
1 oz wasabi capelin roes
1 oz soy sauce

Sushi has been gaining in popularity in the West in recent decades and has of late come into vogue in Iceland. Sushi depends a lot on fresh ingredients. In this respect Iceland comes in strong, as fresh and firm fish is very easy to come by, the Icelanders being a forefront fishing nation.

Begin by blanching the monkfish for a very short time and then cut the meat into thin slices. Make a small bed of seaweed salad seasoned with a few drops of soy sauce and place the monkfish on top. To finish the dish off, set a dollop of wasabi-flavored capelin roes atop the monkfish.

This fresh and pleasant dish is best served in medium sized soup spoons, four spoons per serving. The firm texture and pleasing flavor of the monkfish is wonderfully enhanced by the wasabi-marinated capelin roes.

8 roma tomatoes, blanched (see appendix)
7 oz halibut
8 mussels
4 scallops
4 cups fish stock (see appendix)
1 bunch basil
1 bunch thyme
1 teaspoon black peppercorns
Sprigs of chervil
3 oz cold butter
Salt and pepper

# SEAFOOD SOUP
## with Halibut, Mussel and Scallop

(serves four)

**Begin by blanching** the fresh tomatoes, removing their skin and mixing them in a blender along with the thyme and chervil. For stronger taste, simmer the liquid until it has reduced to half its original volume. Then pass the tomato reduction through a chinoise and add the basil and the fish stock. Cut the cold butter into small pieces and stir it into the soup, adding salt and pepper to taste. The result should be a decidedly red broth.

Steam the mussels until they open. Then remove one of the shells, leaving the fish inside the other one. Cut the halibut into fair-sized pieces and sauté them lightly in butter along with the scallop.

For serving, the soup is put in a soup plate and a mussel, still in the shell, and pieces of the sautéed halibut and scallop put in the soup. The shell should resemble a boat floating in the red soup and the pieces of halibut and scallop reminiscent of islands.

# CLIFFS, FIELDS AND WILD TERRAIN

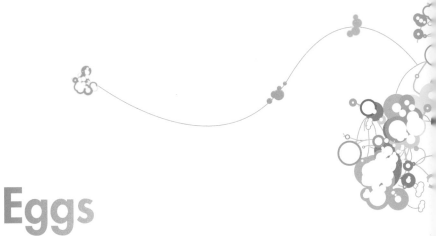

# Eggs

**Besides eggs from hens, Icelanders have always used the eggs of wild birds for food; mainly the eggs of sea birds, which hatch in the steep cliffs found in many places around the country.**

**Sea bird** eggs were collected in the tens of thousands and often eaten fresh, either cooked or raw, but it was impossible to consume immediately the great quantity collected.

One method used for preservation was to keep the eggs in sea weed ash or peat sheds, taking care to keep air from getting to them. A similar method was to ferment the eggs, mainly the half-hatched ones, in ash from dried sheep droppings. In both cases the eggs were boiled thoroughly before eating. They could also be hard-boiled, removed from the shell, and put into sour whey; or preserved in a special mixture called egg brine, which was made of salt and chalk dissolved in water.

**Nowadays,** we might find eggs kept thus spoiled and perhaps unfit for eating, but these storage methods show the ingenuity of the old Icelanders in solving food-preservation problems which I, for one, find laudable.

# Gathering
## sea bird eggs

Iceland is a very mountainous country, with usable farmland making up only a small part of its terrain. In a great many places the mountains reach all the way out to the sea, where they end in either large and impassable rockslides or break off abruptly in towering cliffs roaring to the heavens in perpendicular rock faces, where only the seabirds find foothold on narrow sills or small outcrops to hatch their eggs.

In the spring of 2004 I was lucky to get the opportunity to go egg gathering on the cliffs of Langanes in the north-east. I and my travelling companions arrived in Þórshöfn (Thor's Harbor) and sought out our guides, experts in cliffmanship. Together we got into all-terrain vehicles and drove along a truly horrendous road past beaches covered with driftwood and scattered with abandoned farmhouses. The latter were a saddening sight. Our minds wandered back to the people who once lived there wrenching their livelihoods from the harsh land and the sea that incessantly lapped at the boulders lining the shore.

Finally, after innumerable bumps and bounces, we arrived at the cliffs. We unloaded our gear in the vicinity of a nice summer cottage, which serves the cliff men every spring, when they go egg gathering.

**After one** of the experts had gone down the cliff, demonstrating how it is done, I donned the harness, fastened myself to the rope, and was lowered down. The method is similar to the one used in the old days, except I was lowered using a bollard welded to the bumper of a large vehicle. This seemed pretty safe to me, and though I have to admit I was a little uneasy, down I went, landing on a rather wide ledge with the cliff towering over me and the sea roaring below. Soon more men joined me and off we went gathering eggs, which were lying in great numbers on the barren rock. All we had to do was pick them up and put them in the bags in our clothing, but it was hazardous work, for the ledge was extremely slippery from wet bird droppings and sea slime. Slipping, I knew, could easily mean falling headlong into the swirling breakers beating at the cliff.

When our bags would hold no more eggs, up we went again. This was done by attaching the rope to the bumper of the vehicle and slowly backing it up. Once on top of the cliff, we emptied our bags, removed the eggs that had been accidentally broken, and put the others in vessels fit to bring them off the cliff.

**This was** undeniably an amazing experience, but it left me a bit spent. I'd sweated profusely and was certainly pleased to again be on firm ground, where I was sure of my footing. Soon, though, I managed to regain my everyday composure, in which I was greatly assisted through the consumption of some raw eggs drunk straight from the shells. They were great in taste and marvellously complimented the rugged surroundings, the fresh wind blowing in my hair, and the continuing and spectacular symphony of the breaking seas and the shrieking sea birds fluttering in the air.

# Flat Bread

Very probably the Icelandic "flatbrauð" (flat bread) is particular to the country. It has long been a food staple there, made in roughly the same manner through the centuries. The flour most used for flat bread is rye mixed with hot water and a little salt. But through the ages, when flour in general was hard to come by, various other ingredients were added, such as lymegrass flour, ground Iceland moss, and fish roe. In latter times wheat was used, as well as oatmeal.

The dough is kneaded into a firm, uniform ball, which is cut into bits. These are rolled out into long sticks of dough, which are sliced into disks sufficient in size for each cake. The disks are then flattened into a circular shape with a rolling pin, all the cakes ending up the same size.

In the olden times the cakes of flat bread were baked on the embers of the cooking fire, turned over now and then, and the soot and ash brushed off. Nowadays the cakes are baked either on a very hot plate, which is considered the better method, or singed with a hand-held gas burner. The latter method tends to leave the cakes a bit raw and sticky.

Flat bread is very delicious indeed. It is eaten with lots of butter, which is the way I really like it, especially when it is fresh and still warm. Also, different kinds of garnish go well with flat bread, such as slices of smoked meat, smoked salmon, cheese and so on.

2 cups of plain white flour
1 tablespoon sugar
3 eggs
Milk, as needed
2 oz margarine
Half a teaspoon baking soda
Chunky mango sauce (see appendix)

# ICELANDIC CREPES
## filled with Whipped Cream on Chunky Mango Sauce

No coffee or tea party in Iceland is complete without crepes; they're practically a staple, and will be found wherever people gather for pleasant conversation and friendship. This is easy to understand, as Icelandic crepes are very easy to make and absolutely delicious.

Put all the ingredients in a bowl and mix thoroughly until the mixture has become nearly as fluid as milk. Ladle some of the mixture onto a shallow, sizzling hot pan and swirl it around until the dough covers its entire surface. Pour any excess mixture back into the bowl. Bake the crepe until it is almost dry on top and then turn it, using a long-bladed spatula, and bake a bit more. It should be golden brown on both sides when done.

The crepes are mainly served in two ways. One technique is to put a good splash of firmly whipped cream on one fourth of the crepe and then folding it twice. Sometimes a bit of rhubarb or blueberry jam is put on the crepe along with the whipped cream. The other method is to scatter quite a bit of sugar on the crepe while it's still hot and then roll it up tightly. The sugar melts within the roll and seeps through it, making it quite syrupy. Either of the two ways gives fine results, but other fillings can work well, such as cheese, jelly, chopped fresh fruit and so on.

The picture on the opposite page shows one of the alternative methods possible for serving the crepes. In it the crepe is not folded, but formed into a bag around the filling, which can be whipped cream, cream cheese, shrimp salad, and so on, and the bag tied up with a thread from, for example, rhubarb. The bag is put onto a bed of chunky mango sauce.

# LEAF-CUT BREAD

4.4 lb flour

7 oz margarine

3.5 oz sugar

1 teaspoon salt

1 teaspoon baking powder

2.5 pt hot milk

Making Leaf-Cut Bread (laufabrauð) is an old Iceland-ic tradition, very much linked to the preparations for Christmas. Of old, "laufabrauð" was most prevalent in the northern part of Iceland, but nowadays the making of this peculiar, thin kind of very brittle bread is common all over the country in the early weeks of December.

Put all the ingredients into a fairly large bowl and mix them together thoroughly until firm and uniform. Then scatter some flour on top of the kitchen counter and empty the dough onto it. Knead the dough by hand until it's completely smooth and free of all cracks.

Section the dough into five or six even pieces. Form each piece into a roll about two inches in diameter. Put the rolls in a tray side by side, cover them with a clean kitchen towel, close the tray with a sheet of plastic wrap, and place the dough overnight in a cool place.

When you're ready to make the bread, scatter some flour on top of the kitchen counter and cut a slice of dough, about half an inch to an inch in thickness. Place the slice, cut end down, in the flour and roll it out with a rolling pin until it's so thin you can almost read through it.

When the rolling is done, place a round, eight-inch plate upside down on the rolled-out dough, and cut along its edge. Remove the excess dough and lift off the plate. Then gently lift the circular cake off the counter and put it aside on a sheet of paper towel, with a second sheet of towel on top. Repeat the above process, forming stacks of fifteen to twenty cakes. The total yield should be seventy to eighty cakes.

The cakes are decorated before they're fried, so they mustn't be too moist. If they are, break up a stack and spread out the cakes to dry a bit. When the moisture is right, place a cake on a wooden platter and, with a small, well-sharpened knife, make V-shaped cuts in it, forming rows resembling a feather. The cuts should be about one-eighth of an inch apart. The rows of cuts can take any form possible: letters or figures or whatever comes to mind. When the cutting is through, bend over the tip of the first upside-down V and press down, exposing a tip. Then bend down the second V and press it down on the tip exposed by the first one, and so on until all the rows have been worked in this way.

The cutting is a somewhat time-consuming process, but is really the most pleasant part in the preparation of the Leaf-Cut Bread. In it, imagination, creativity and originality have free rein. In this work all the members of the family, and frequently relatives and friends, too, take part, good-humoredly competing in who can create the best and most fanciful decorations.

When the cakes have been cut, the frying can begin. Put the individual cakes in very hot oil and fry until they're golden in color. When ready, fish out a cake and place it flat on a layer of paper towels and put a wooden platter on top to make it flat. Fry the next cake. When it's ready, remove the one being flattened and put the just-fried one in its place, platter on top. When the baking is through and the cakes have become cool, put each stack in a tightly-closed container and place it in cool storage to await the Christmas festivities.

# Ale

It's known that the Icelanders of old, at a time when barley was grown in the country, brewed their own ale. But the process has continued over the centuries, even though barley has to be imported.

Ale was brewed from germinated barley. When the germination had reached the desired stage, the barley was dried, preferably in the sun, and when dry enough, ground in special mills. The ground barley was immersed in water for some time, sometimes with juniper and bark for taste, and hops for preservation. After an appropriate period, the mixture was poured into hot water and stirred vigorously to free the sugar. Finally, the liquid was poured through a strainer into a barrel and some yeast added.

**During the fermentation** the barrel was kept closed, except for the removal of the froth formed. When the fermentation process was over, the ale was poured into another barrel and left to settle and cure for several days, after which it was fit for drinking.

Ale, or beer, was not made or sold in Iceland for decades in the twentieth century. Not so long ago (1989) the ban on the production and selling of the beverage was lifted and now beer is again made in Iceland, for the most part commercially, but also a little in the home.

# Dandelion Wine

Since no grapes grow in Iceland, except in hothouses, we didn't have grape wine in the country until the nation was Christianized in the year 1000, when it began to be imported for use in church communion ceremonies.

In the north-eastern part of Iceland, however, small quantities of wine were produced using the dandelion flower. The technique is ancient and rather simple.

A layer of sugar was put in the bottom of a barrel and a layer of flowers put on top. The flowers were covered with another layer of sugar, and then another layer of flowers and so on. When the layers had accumulated to the depth of about a foot, water at about body temperature was poured into the barrel, covering the layers of sugar and dandelion flowers completely.

Fermentation started of its own accord and lasted for six to eight weeks, during which time sugar was added, if needed. At the end of fermentation, the brew was poured through a piece of, for example, linen cloth, the barrel cleaned, and the wine poured into it again for curing. This part of the process lasted for several months, after which the wine was either drunk or put in bottles for storage.

I was fortunate enough to know one of the foremost dandelion wine makers in my area and was even allowed to watch his winemaking. He used the same arrangement in filling the barrel as the one above, but the method for measuring the ingredients was his own. So he put a handful of this, a dash of that, a pinch of the third, and a drop of the fourth and so on. In spite of this rather unscientific approach, the outcome he obtained was always excellent. Especially important, I remember, was the drop of dew that had gathered in a flower during Midsummer Night. This he put in last, making the sign of the cross over the barrel, and told me that this small drop of heavenly liquid was the weightiest item in the making of a good brew.

Dandelion wine is really very good. I've tasted it several times. Of course there is some difference between various batches, depending on the wine maker, but in all instances the Icelandic dandelion wine I have sampled has been most pleasant.

2 cups Iceland moss
1 cup cooked rice
4.2 pints whole milk
1 pint sour milk
Sugar
Salt

# ICELAND
# MOSS CURDS
(serves four)

Iceland moss (Cetraria islandica) is a low-lying plant which forms easily identifiable patches in many highland and heathery areas. For ages this humble growth has been collected for food in Iceland, though not quite continuously, as the moss almost completely died out in a great volcanic eruption in the eighteenth century when sulfuric ash covered the island, spoiling vegetation and killing both livestock and people.

Begin by boiling the rice in water with a little salt until the rice has become soft. Strain off excess water.

Put the milk into a fairly large pot. Then add the sour milk and stir the mixture with a wooden spoon for a total blend. When this has been done, put the pot on the stove and heat it until the mixture is almost boiling.

When all the milk has curdled, remove the curdles with a skimmer and put them aside in a bowl. The remaining liquid should resemble whey in color.

Wash the moss in cold water, chop it into pieces about an inch in length, and put it in the pot with the liquid from the curdling, along with the cooked rice, and heat the mixture until it's almost boiling.

Finally, chop the curds into bits about half an inch in diameter and add these to the hot broth. Season to taste with salt and sugar.

At first this soup may look unappetizing, but be assured its flavor is exceptional. It's also packed with vitamins, making it a very healthy dish.

# Wild Thyme

Wild thyme is a beautiful plant with small, lavender-coloured flowers. It grows where the ground is not very fertile and is found all over Iceland both in the lowlands and in the highlands.

Wild thyme was used quite a lot in Iceland in the old days, mostly for tea, and also for flavoring. This is still the case nowadays, but in the old days the plant was also thought to be of medical importance and was used quite a lot in home-made medicine.

# Juniper

Juniper is rather common in Iceland. The berries are not eaten much when fresh, but in the old days they were often burnt in an oven or in a pot and ground for a drink reminiscent of coffee. Also the berries were used for flavouring drinks such as wine, and thought to have healing power for, for example, chest pain.

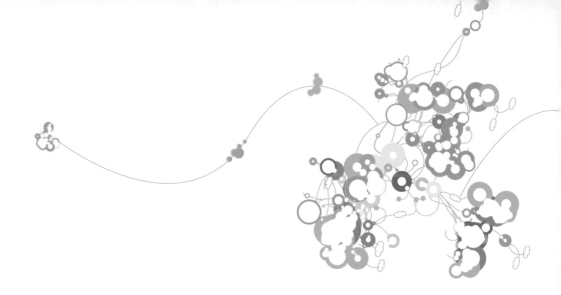

# Blueberries
## and Crowberries

The berries most common in Iceland are blueberries and crowberries.

In the old days berries were preserved in sugar. A layer of berries was put on the bottom of a vessel and sugar strewn on top to cover it. Another layer of berries was added and then more sugar, and so on. The result was a kind of syrup, very sweet and full in taste. A peculiar use was sometimes made of the blueberry juice. It was kept for a while to sour, and then the liquid was used for the treatment of animal skin.

## APPLE AND BLUE
## CHEESE SALAD

7 oz blue cheese
1 apple
2.9 oz walnut
Walnut vinaigrette (see appendix)
10 oz mixed green salad

For the salad, peel the apple and then cut it into very narrow strips. Then break the chunk of blue cheese into small bits and place them in a bowl along with the strips of apple, the walnut vinaigrette and the green salad. Gently toss these ingredients together.

Toast the walnuts in an oven tray at 350°F/175°C for about fifteen minutes and then crunch them into bits; not too fine, though, as it is preferable to feel their crunchiness, when eating the salad.

To serve, place a fair heap of the salad in the center of a plate. Scatter the crunched walnuts quite liberally on top.

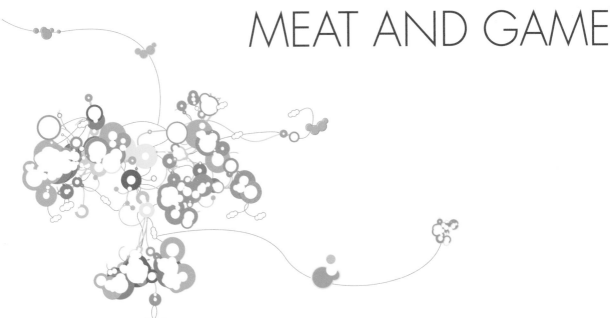

# Icelandic Sheep

I was brought up in the country and at the age of eleven I became a part-time farmhand at a local farm. Some of my fondest memories are of going with the farmer to the sheep houses in the wintertime and helping him bring the hay from the barn and distributing it in the long mangers that ran the length of each house. Those were happy times.

Just as pleasant were the rides we took on the sure-footed and versatile Icelandic horses as we drove the sheep out of the lower valleys and up into the mountains for summer grazing, well away from all pollution. There they were left to roam unhampered all summer long among clear fresh-water streams, lofty peaks and glaciers. This is still the general practice and the complete freedom and total absence of any human interference means the sheep are free to use their natural instincts to seek out the most succulent grasses and tastiest herbs to be found in their highland pastures. Because of this they truly are wildlife; and their meat acquires a particularly savoury flavour not found in any other meat.

# one

One of the most fascinating events on an Icelandic farm occurs in the autumn, when the sheep are brought down from the mountains. Then legions of horse-riding men gather the sheep into huge flocks. This is frequently a task encompassing a number of days, so tents and food are brought along on pack horses. When all the sheep have been gathered, the entire herd is driven into the valleys. It's truly a spellbinding and unforgettable sight to see them cascading down the slopes, resembling immense and frothy waterfalls.

**The culmination** of the sheep-gathering is the driving of the sheep into a huge enclosure made up of a large centre part encircled by numerous smaller ones, each belonging to an individual farmer. This is usually accompanied by a lot of shouting and running and grabbing, as the farmers and their helpers single out their sheep and drag them into the appropriate enclosures. This is the sheep farmers' harvest day, with people gathering from near and far to take part in the festivities, singing, telling tales, meeting friends, joking, laughing and dancing far into the night, until finally each farmer mounts his horse again and drives his herd home to the farm.

# RED WINE-BRAISED LAMB SHANK
## with Semolina Cake
### (serves four)

4 braised lamb shanks and reduced
lamb sauce (see appendix)
3 tablespoons olive oil
½ cup carrots, peeled and cut on the bias
½ cup white pearl onions, peeled and blanched
½ cup parsnips, peeled and diced small
½ cup celery root, peeled and cut on the bias
2 cloves garlic, peeled and minced
1 ½ cups milk
1 cup water
¾ cup semolina flour
¼ cup grated parmesan cheese
1 egg yolk
2 tablespoons chopped rosemary
24 pickled rosemary leaves
Salt and pepper

Every year in the spring the lamb in northern Iceland are moved to the mountain plains in order to graze on the wild herbs and greens. In September the lamb is herded and brought back down to the plains for butchering. The vegetation of the highland terrain gives the meat a strong and wild flavor.

To prepare the vegetable: Using 2 tablespoons of olive oil, sauté the carrots in a medium sauté pan on medium heat. Once the carrots are cooked halfway add the pearl onions, parsnips, and celery root. Cook the vegetables until they are golden brown. In another pot combine the reduced lamb sauce and the sautéed vegetables. Season with salt and pepper.

To prepare the semolina cakes: In a medium size pot, over medium heat, sauté the onion and garlic in 1 tablespoon of olive oil. Once they are soft add the milk and water. Bring to a boil and season with salt and pepper until the mixture is heavily seasoned. While whisking, slowly pour in the semolina flour until the mixture is completely incorporated. Keep whisking for 3-5 minutes. Add the parmesan cheese, and rosemary. Remove the pan from the heat and using a wooden spoon, fold in the egg yolk until it is incorporated. Evenly pour out on to a parchment paper-lined tray and refrigerate. Once it is completely chilled cut out four circles. Sauté the cakes in a non-stick pan until they are golden brown and crispy on both sides. Keep warm until ready to serve.

Assembly: Place the crispy semolina cake in the middle of the plate. Lean the braised lamb shank on the semolina cake. Spoon the sautéed vegetables and sauce around and on top of the lamb. Garnish with picked rosemary leaves.

# SAUTÉED
# FILLET OF LAMB
## with Purple and Fingerling Potatoes, Baby Carrots and Lamb Reduction

**(serves four)**

1.8 lb fillet of lamb
4 tablespoons grape seed oil
1 tablespoon butter
5 sprigs thyme
1 clove garlic
1 sprig rosemary
4 oz fingerling potatoes
4 oz purple potatoes
12 baby carrots
2 cups lamb stock (see appendix)

Trim the fillet of lamb and season it with salt and pepper. After letting the fillet rest for a short time (for the seasoning to seep in), place it in a hot pan with a little oil and sauté it on all sides until it is quite brown. Toward the end of the sautéing, add the butter, thyme, garlic and rosemary to the pan and roll the fillet through the fat and seasoning. Next, put the fillet into an oven heated to 350°F/175°C, and roast it for about two minutes. Remove the fillet from the oven and leave it for about five minutes for the heat to sink in. Return the meat to the oven again for two minutes more, remove and rest again for five minutes, and finally return it to the oven for an additional two minutes. During each resting period, turn the meat occasionally to regulate the flow of juices within the fillet.

Boil the potatoes until they're soft. (It is preferable that all the potatoes are roughly the same size) Remove the potatoes from the water and squash them with a spatula to the thickness of about a quarter of an inch. Season the potatoes with salt and pepper and sauté them in grape seed oil.

Peel the carrots and roast them for twenty minutes in an oven at 300°F/150°C. The carrots must be turned now and then to ensure even roasting.

For the sauce put the lamb stock in a pot and reduce it by half. Then add two tablespoons of butter and whisk it in thoroughly to soften the sauce. Season it to taste with salt and pepper.

To serve, arrange a bed of fingerling and purple potatoes in the center of a plate. Cut the finished fillet of lamb into thin slices and place them decoratively on top of the potatoes, highlighting the arrangement with three roasted carrots. Lines of sauce are put on the plate forming a square around the arrangement and some more sauce served on the side.

# Cooking on earth´s fire

Volcanoes abound in Iceland and, though most of them are considered extinct, a good number are decidedly not so, such as the volcano under the ice cap of Vatnajökull (Lakes' Ice Cap) in the south-east, Mount Askja in the East and the famed Mount Hekla in the South, formerly believed to be one of the gateways to Hell.

**It so happened** that I was at home in Iceland the last time Mount Hekla erupted. It was winter, with a lot of snow on the ground, and the weather not so good. I decided to act on an idea of mine, which was to try to cook on molten lava. I mentioned this to a few friends of mine, who owned various kinds of four wheel drive vehicles. At first they suggested that I'd finally gone completely around the bend. They thought that going to take a look at the eruption was a splendid idea, but cooking on the lava was something they considered quite idiotic.

Still, off we went, carrying various survival kits and bringing quite a lot of meat and vegetables along with a copper pot and other necessities for my attempt at cooking. The trip took several hours, with the last stretch quite heavy going over a heavy layer of snow.

As we got closer to the volcano we could see the great billows of smoke filled with ashes and flying rocks emitting from the fiery craters, and when we finally stopped, turned off the engines, and stepped out of our vehicles, the roar of the mighty powers being unleashed in front of our very eyes hit our ears with all their deafening and horrendous force.

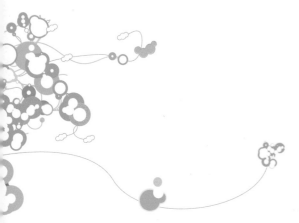

**We were** at the very edge of the lava, which rolled over the ground in a huge, black wall of virgin rock and incessantly hurled down red-hot boulders revealing the glowing semi-liquid rock inside. I must admit I was a bit scared; this was a little more than I'd anticipated. But I was still set on carrying out my plan. So taking out my equipment and the food I intended to cook, I gingerly approached a spot where the molten rock protruded from the black and cooling surface. I was wearing what protective attire I could muster, which was certainly needed. A heavy wind was blowing, but still the heat beaming from the lava wall was so tremendous that I was immediately bathed in sweat and glowing red in the face. I also had to be on a constant lookout for the hot rock slides slithering down the lava wall. Still, I managed to put my pot filled with snow and vegetables in a pretty good spot. The snow melted in an instant and very soon the water was boiling briskly. I started grilling the meat right there on the hot rocks. It sizzled immediately and I had a hard time turning it so that it would not go up in flames and turn into ashes. Some small stones kept bouncing off my back, but fortunately no large ones hit me, though they kept rolling onto the ground at my feet.

**I'm not going** to claim that this meal cooked on earth's virgin fire is the best one I ever made, but the meat and the vegetables tasted fine as I and my companions, who had watched from a safe distance, sat down on the bumpers of our vehicles to partake of it and to enjoy Mother Nature's magnificent show.

# SAUTÉED PORK
# TENDERLOIN
## with Chanterelle Mushrooms, Lentil Beans, and Caramelized Apples

(serves four)

1.8 lb pork tenderloin
8.5 oz chanterelle mushrooms
7 oz red beet
20 haricots vert, blanched (see appendix)
1 tablespoon butter
5 sprigs thyme
1 clove garlic, chopped
2 apples
½ cup sugar
2 tablespoons grape seed oil
½ cup balsamic vinegar
Salt and pepper

Cut the red beets into strips about an inch and a half in length and about a quarter of an inch across. Toss the strips in olive oil and place them on an oven tray. Roast the strips at 300°F/150°C, rotating them occasionally to ensure evenness. This should take about twenty minutes.

Season the pork tenderloin with some salt and pepper and sauté the meat in a hot pan with oil. Take care to sauté the meat evenly on all sides until it is golden brown. When this is done, put the meat into an oven preheated to about 350°F/175°C. Keep the meat in the oven for five minutes and then remove it

for five minutes. Repeat the process. After the second time it is wise to inspect the meat by making a cut in it to see if it is done. Over-cooked pork is dry, so this is a fine way to do it well.

While the meat is cooking, use the pan the pork was sautéed in to make apple glaze. For this we put wedges of the peeled apples in the hot pan and sauté them for about three minutes. Next put the sugar in the pan and heat it until it caramelizes, at which time add the balsamic vinegar and cook at low heat for about two minutes.

Now cut both ends off the blanched haricots vert, and sauté them in butter for about thirty seconds. Sauté the mushrooms in a hot pan in the grape seed oil along with the garlic and a few sprigs of the thyme and season with salt and pepper. Remove the thyme from the blend, as it is just used for flavouring.

When the pork tenderloin is done, cut it into slices about a quarter of an inch in thickness. Make a bed in the centre of a plate using the mushrooms and the red beets. Arrange the haricots vert on top of the bed. Finally, place some slices of the pork tenderloin on the bed and pour the apple glaze over the meat. Lay some wedges of caramelized apple on top. This is it; and it is certainly very delicious.

# FILLET OF REINDEER
## with Morel Mushrooms and
## Beet Root Sauce

(serves four)

1.8 lb reindeer fillet
4 egg whites
7 oz crunched mixed nuts
12 medium sized morel mushrooms
1 sprig rosemary
Beet root sauce (see appendix)
2 tablespoons grape seed oil
3.5 oz butter

Reindeer are virtual newcomers to Iceland. They were brought in from Norway in three batches in the second half of the eighteenth century. One batch was let loose in the eastern part of the country and the animals in that shipment were the only ones to survive and multiply. Reindeer meat has a very strong and appealing heathery taste coming from the pastures the animals graze on. They are the only really wild land animals in Iceland that are hunted for food.

In preparing this course, begin by beating the egg whites into a froth and spreading the crunched nuts on a plate. Season the tenderloin of reindeer with salt and pepper, roll it in the beaten egg whites until the meat is totally covered, then shift the tenderloin over to the plate of crunched nuts and thoroughly encrust it.

Next, put some grape seed oil in a medium hot pan and sauté the tenderloin in it until the nuts and the egg whites have turned into a dark-brown shell closing up the meat. When this is accomplished, remove the tenderloin from the pan and put it in an oven, which has been preheated to 350°F/175°C. The tenderloin is left in the oven for five minutes and then removed and left for ten minutes to let the heat seep into the meat. This is done two more times. Through this process the meat gets more evenly cooked than if it is left in the oven continuously the entire time it is cooking.

While the tenderloin is cooking, cut the morel mushrooms in half and sauté them in a hot pan in grape seed oil along with a sprig of rosemary. Toward the end of the sautéing, add some butter to the pan as well as salt and pepper to taste.

When the tenderloin is done, cut it into slices about a quarter of an inch in thickness. Place these on a plate and decorate the arrangement with the morel mushrooms and beet root sauce. As a garnish, any roasted root vegetable can be recommended because of their earthy flavour.

# RABBIT FILLET
## with Rabbit Confit, Shiitake
# Mushrooms and Port Wine Sauce
### (serves four)

2 saddles of rabbit
2 tablespoons grape seed oil
4 rabbit leg confit (see appendix)
4.2 oz shiitake mushrooms
A pinch of sea cress
Port wine sauce (see appendix)
Salt and pepper

A few farmers in Iceland raise rabbits for food. This is a late development, so rabbit meat is rather hard to get in shops and is mainly used in restaurants. But if you can find it, I think you'll find this an excellent rabbit recipe.

Begin by cutting the fillet off the saddle and removing the silver skin. Sauté the fillet in the oil on all sides until golden brown and then flavor it to taste with salt and pepper.

Next, chop the mushrooms into medium sized bits and sauté them in butter.

Now cut the sautéed rabbit fillet into thin slices and arrange them decoratively on a plate. Place the sautéed bits of mushroom around the slices of rabbit fillet. Finally, form a small bunch of heated shredded rabbit leg confit and put it on top of the slices of rabbit fillet. Finally the sea cress is added for decoration.

Now you're ready to present your achievement to your guests. This is a rather small portion, so it's recommended that you increase the amounts proportionally for larger servings.

# CRISPY
# MOULARD DUCK
# BREAST

## with Braised Red Cabbage, Duck Confit Tortellini and Walnut Vinaigrette

**(serves four)**

2 moulard duck breasts, trimmed, with the skin scored

5 tablespoons butter

1 red onion, peeled and sliced

2 cloves garlic, peeled and minced

3 cups red cabbage, shredded

1 cup merlot wine

1 cup ruby port

1 bay leaf

Pasta (see appendix)

¾ cup Duck Confit meat, shredded (see appendix)

6 tablespoons Walnut Vinaigrette (see appendix)

20 fresh tarragon leaves

Salt and pepper

**The duck in Iceland** is incredible! Slowly rendering the skin crispy gives a deep, caramelized, meaty flavor, the sharp mustard sauce cuts right through the soft buttery cabbage, and the little plump tortellini are heavenly.

To prepare the duck: Season the two duck breasts liberally with salt and pepper. Place the seasoned duck in a medium to low heat sauté pan, skin side down. There will be more than enough fat from the skin to prevent the breast from sticking. Slowly cook the breast until it's golden brown and crispy.

Turn the breasts over and cook for 2-3 minutes more. Remove the duck from the pan and let it rest 15 minutes before slicing.

To prepare the cabbage: In a medium size pot, heat 2 tablespoons of butter until it starts to foam. Add the red onion and garlic and cook until it's translucent. Next, add the red cabbage and stir it continuously until the cabbage has wilted. Pour in the merlot and port and bring to a low simmer. Add the bay leaf and let the mixture braise for approximately 35 minutes or until the cabbage is tender and the liquid is almost entirely reduced. Season with salt and pepper and finish the cabbage by folding in 2 tablespoons of butter until it's creamy.

To prepare the tortellini: Cut the pasta sheets into 16 1½ inch squares. Place one teaspoon of Duck Confit meat onto each square. Lightly brush the outside of each pasta square with egg wash. Fold the square into a triangle and gently press the edges together. Bring the two far corners together, pinching them in place. After each tortellini is finished place them on a floured tray and refrigerate until ready to cook.

Just before plating the dish cook the tortellini in boiling, salted water for 4 minutes. Remove them from the water and toss with the remaining tablespoon of butter.

Assembly: Place 2 tablespoons of the braised cabbage in the middle of the plate. Next, place the sliced duck breast on top of the cabbage. Place the tortellini around the duck, using the cabbage to prevent it from sliding. Spoon the mustard sauce around the plate and garnish with the tarragon leaves.

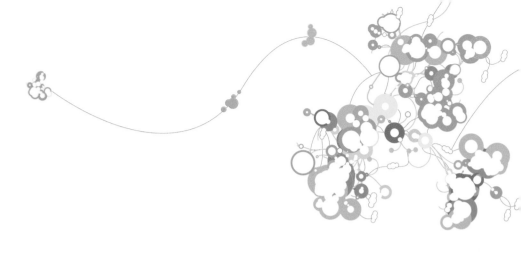

# SHEEP DUNG
## or Peat-Smoked Meat

For centuries in Iceland, before modern methods were developed, smoking was the preferred method of preserving meat. Lamb or pork, for example, was hung in the rafters of a cooking house, where an open fire was always kept burning, and the smoke allowed to envelope the meat before escaping through a hole in the roof.

The taste produced was, of course, affected by the particular fuel used, the most popular choices being peat or dried sheep dung. Of the two, the one commonly thought to give the most pleasing taste was the sheep dung. This fuel is still the one most frequently used for the smoking of meat in Iceland, but birch, which gives a somewhat different taste, is also common.

# milk

Icelandic cows are a special breed, brought to the country by the early settlers about eleven hundred years ago, and since then there's been almost no interbreeding with other species of cattle. In times past every farmer in Iceland tried to keep a cow or two, whose milk is said to be especially wholesome, for example having ingredients which work against diabetes.

**In the old days** most of the milk was poured into rather wide and shallow receptacles and left for a day or two. The cream rose to the surface in the receptacles, and was either skimmed off, or, if the receptacle was supplied with a small, plugged hole at the bottom, the skim milk let run off, leaving the cream in the receptacle.

Some of the cream was used for drinking, but the vast majority of it was used for butter, and the skimmed milk for drinking, cooking and further processing.

2 pt cow beestings
1 pt whole milk
Cinnamon sugar
Salt

# Curds
# of Beestings
## with Cinnamon Sugar

(serves four)

The milk from a cow in the first several days after calving was generally thought unfit for immediate consumption, either for drinking or for the production of cream or butter. Still, it wasn't thrown out, but used to make curds.

Mix the beestings and the milk together thoroughly, adding salt to taste.

When the blend has become uniform, pour it into a jar or jug. Place the vessel into a pot and pour water into the pot until it reaches to about halfway up the outside of the vessel. Bring the water to a boil and heat the mixture of beestings and milk until it forms into a kind of pudding. When it has become quite firm, remove the vessel from the pot of water, and the curds of beestings are complete.

The curds are served in a soup plate and most often eaten with milk poured around them. Various juices, such as blueberry, are also very fitting. The curds are velvety and mellow in taste. They're most often eaten with a dash of cinnamon sugar on top.

This food is still popular in Iceland, but not as common as in the old days, since the beestings are hard to come by. They are not sold in shops, so one really must know a cow farmer to acquire them.

# Cheese

Cheese was made on the farms in Iceland in the first centuries of settlement in the country. Cheese making, however, got gradually rarer, and became almost non-existent in the late middle ages, except in the Eastern Fjords. At present a great variety of cheeses are made in Iceland, and, in fact, Icelandic cheese makers have done very well in international competitions.

# Skyr

**Skimmed milk was used quite a lot for drinking and cooking, but a good part of what was produced was utilized for the making of "skyr".**

For "skyr" the skimmed milk was heated almost to a boiling point, and then poured into a vessel and let cool. Rennet, usually made from dry, un-soured skyr, mixed with milk or cream and a piece of a calf's stomach, was added to the cooled skimmed milk, and the mixture stirred vigorously for a complete blend. When the mixture started curdling, cuts were made in it for the whey to seep into. Finally, when the curdling was over, the skyr was put on a rack placed over a vessel and left for the whey to drip off.

1 lb skyr
½ cup water or milk
Milk or cream
Sugar to taste

# SKYR
## topped with Blueberries
**(serves four)**

"Skyr," a delicacy singular to Iceland, has definitely not gotten the recognition it deserves among the gourmands of the world and may be difficult to find outside of Iceland, where it is greatly appreciated and, indeed, has been for centuries.

Skyr in its natural state is quite dry and firm, so most people feel that it must be softened somewhat before consumption. This is done by stirring some liquid into it, either pure water, milk or a mixture of milk and cream. The resulting mixture should be velvety, very white, and have the consistency of very heavy yogurt or porridge. Some sugar is often added to taste, and the skyr served in a soup plate with milk or cream.

Various fruits are often mixed with the stirred skyr, such as blueberries, crowberries, or chopped fruit such as strawberries, apples, pears, bananas and so on, which all go marvellously with skyr.

Skyr, only stirred with a spot of sugar, is the favourite breakfast food of many Icelanders. Children take a box of skyr, flavoured or plain, with them to school. Some like to keep the skyr for some time to let it go sour. Whichever way, this food item is delicious, non-fattening, filling and rich in various substances such as protein and calcium.

# BRENNIVÍN BABA
## with Créme Anglaise

(serves four)

### For the Baba

¼ oz package yeast
2 tablespoons sugar
2 tablespoons warm water
4 tablespoons butter
¼ cup milk
Pinch of salt
2 eggs
2 cups sifted all-purpose flour
Crème anglaise (see appendix)

### For the Brennivín Syrup

1 cup water
1 cup sugar
½ cup brennivín

When we speak of baba, we most often have the rum variety in mind. Still, it's really up to the individual baker to decide which spirits are used. Also, in the list of ingredients above, lemon is stipulated, though other juicy fruits could quite sensibly be used. In this case, we're going to make babas the Icelandic way, using the Icelandic 40% proof "Brennivín" (Burning wine), which also is called "Svarti dauði" (Black Death), for the spirits to make the syrup.

Using a small bowl, combine the yeast, the sugar and the two tablespoons of warm water and stir to dissolve the yeast. Next, put the butter and the milk in a small saucepan and heat to melt the butter and then cool the mixture to room temperature. Now, beat the eggs with a wire whisk until they're light and a bit frothy.

Next, add the yeast and sugar mixture along with the milk and butter mixture to the eggs and mix the ingredients well. When this liquid is ready, stir in the flour using a wooden spoon to form dough. When this is accomplished, knead the dough by hand in the bowl for 5 minutes, or until it's even in consistency and detaches from the side of the bowl. Then form the dough into a ball, sprinkle it with about two table-spoons of flour, and cover the bowl with a damp towel. Let the dough rise for one and a half to two hours, or until it has doubled in volume.

Take out the baba molds and butter them thoroughly on the inside. Put a portion of the baba dough into each mold, filling each to one third of its volume. Cover the molds with a kitchen towel and let the dough rise in the molds for one hour. When the babas have risen, put them in an oven preheated to 350° F / 175°C and bake them for twenty-five minutes. At the end of the baking, remove the babas from the oven, cool them for five to ten minutes, and then remove them from their molds.

While the dough is rising and the babas baking, make the Brennivín syrup. For this put the cup of water in a saucepan, add the cup of sugar and heat the mixture to melt the sugar, taking care that it does not turn brown. Then, remove the pan from the heat and let the sugar solution cool. Finally, pour the brennivín into the pan, stirring well for an even blend. When the mixture is ready, brush it onto the babas, until the Brennivín syrup has been completely absorbed and they've become soggy with it.

Now the babas are finished. They should be very fragrant, soft and moist, and are to be served cold. One idea is to pour some crème anglaise into a shallow bowl and place a baba in the middle of the pool. Also, firm whipped cream is a fine relish with this most savoury dessert delicacy.

# Þorrablót

**"Þorri" (thorri) is the name of one of the months in the old Icelandic calendar. It began in the 13th week of winter (19th-26th January), and ended in the 18th week of winter (18th-25th February).**

It's likely that the ancient Scandinavians feasted gloriously at the beginning of "þorri" as they celebrated the lengthening of the day and there's evidence that since the early eighteenth century such feasts were held among the well-to-do in Iceland.

Toward the end of the nineteenth century public servants and intellectuals in Iceland revived the "þorrablót" feasts, although they didn't come into general vogue until about the middle of the twentieth century, when some restaurateurs began serving þorri food to their customers. Soon after, it became customary for regional societies, unions of various kinds, inhabitants in small communities, and so on to organize þorrablót. Now this old tradition is very popular in Iceland, and has become a fixture in the social life of the nation.

The food selection at þorrablót is varied, but mainly consists of traditional Icelandic fare: smoked meat, flat or scallop-cut bread, sour food of various kinds, mashed potatoes and mashed Swedish turnips, along with spirits, such as quite liberal amounts of the Icelandic Brennivín (Burning wine). But at þorrablót you will also find some of Iceland's most distinctive and memorable dishes, such as rot-cured shark, singed sheep heads, blood and liver pudding, and ram's testicles.

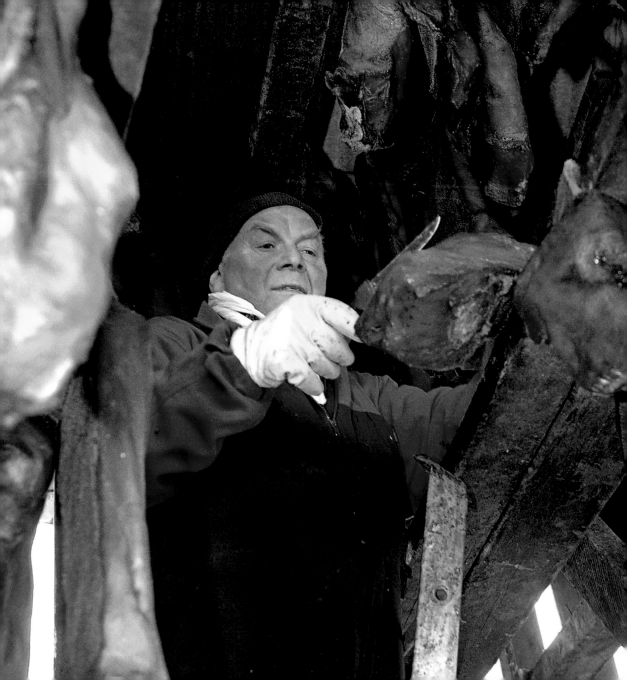

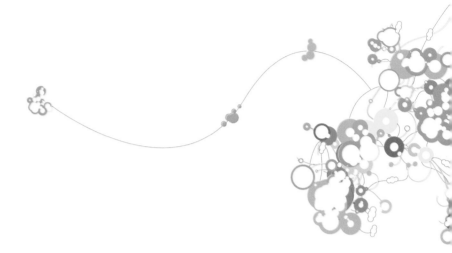

# Rot-Cured Shark

I love this pungent delicacy and always look forward to sampling it, but because Icelandic rot-cured shark, or "hákarl", is made from the Greenland shark, whose raw flesh is highly toxic, great care must be taken in its preparation. Making the meat fit for consumption is a lengthy but necessary process.

**It starts** with flaying the skin off the animal and removing its intestines. Then the meat is cut off in strips about three to four inches across and one and a half to two feet in length.

If the shark has been caught in the wintertime, which is considered the best season for shark, the strips of meat are put in holes on a beach of fine gravel close enough to the shore for ebb and tide to wash through them and the meat left to ferment for three to four months. (If caught in the summertime, the meat is buried between layers of earth) The shark is then dug up and the bits hung and left to ferment in a warm area, until one can penetrate them with a finger. Finally, the bits are hung up in a drying shed to finish the process.

When the treatment is complete, the outside of the meat is quite hard. It is removed to get at the inside, which should be soft and either white or having a yellow, opaque appearance. The former variety is called "skyr-shark" and the latter "glass-shark". The smell of well-cured shark is similar to that of ammonia and perhaps a bit reminiscent of urine. Hence, the absurd and completely untrue tale told to credulous foreigners that, during the curing of the shark meat, it was customary to urinate on it.

In addition to the flesh, many other parts of the shark were also used for food. The cartilage, flippers, and tail were boiled and then cured in sour whey or boiled into hash with fat, such as suet or tallow, stirred in thoroughly, and eaten either hot or as paté with, for example, bread. The shark bears live offspring, which are hatched from eggs inside the animal. When found in the female shark, these eggs were cooked in a fashion similar to other eggs and for the most part eaten hot.

The liver of the shark is very large and contains a lot of fat. The oil extracted from the liver was thought to be especially wholesome and the first thing some people in the old days did each day was to take a hefty sip of shark liver oil. The oil was also a very valuable export commodity, with hundreds of barrels being shipped abroad each year. There the shark liver oil was extensively used for lighting, and it is said that for decades the streets of Copenhagen, Denmark were illuminated with shark liver oil imported from Iceland.

# Singed
## Sheep Head

I've often found that people visiting Iceland, on being introduced to Icelandic cuisine, find the mere appearance of a singed head of lamb rather repellent, and the thought of partaking of the thing almost unthinkable. Over the years, I've come to accept this reaction and to a certain extent even rationalize it.

**The greyish-brown** colour of the boiled head, with the eyes often only partly closed and the teeth showing between somewhat sneering lips, is not the most alluring sight for the gourmand weak of heart. But I know this course is a most savoury one and should much rather be given a sporting chance than rejected untried.

After the head has been removed from the lamb, it is left to cool and cure for some time. In the olden days, the head was then put on a metal fork and held in a blazing fire. A number of times the head was withdrawn from the fire and the singed hair brushed off and the head singed again. A red-hot rod of iron was used to treat places hard to get at, such as the inside of the ears and nostrils. Nowadays hand-held gas burners are utilized for singeing and the rod of iron most often dispensed with.

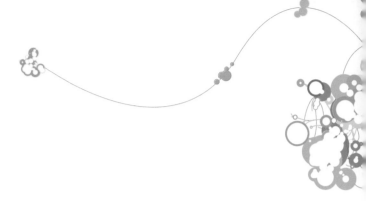

After the singeing, the head is cleaned thoroughly to remove all remains of burnt hair and then sawed in half lengthwise. The brain is removed and the head, especially one of older sheep, is put into storage, formerly in brine but nowadays in a deep freezer.

I find singed head of lamb a very pleasant course indeed. I always boil it in plenty of water and serve it either hot or cold with mashed potatoes and/or mashed Swedish turnips. The meat on the head has a strong and full flavor, but the singeing gives it a pleasing, mellow tinge which reaches through the skin and lingers caressingly on the palate.

A by-line of the above is the singeing of the outer-most part of the sheep foot. The singeing process is the same. The singed feet are cooked until the meat is loose on the bone. Then one either sucks the meat off while hot, savouring the mild and enticing flavor, or scrapes the hot meat from the bones, puts it into a vessel, preferably a square one, and lets it cool and set into an aspic, which is either eaten cold or cured in sour whey. Formerly, and sometimes nowadays, the cooled-off legs were put in sour whey and left there until even the bones were soft and edible. This last treatment is rather rare, but highly valued by some exacting gourmands in my home country.

# Blood Pudding
## / Liver Pudding

**The Icelandic word "slátur" (innards) includes both blood pudding and liver pudding, which are both very popular in Iceland.**

For blood pudding, the blood from sheep is mixed with rye, oatmeal, some water and chopped suet. For liver pudding, liver, and sometimes kidneys too, is ground carefully and then mixed with oatmeal, wheat, some milk and chopped suet. For both, the mixture is put in bags made from the stomachs of sheep and boiled in plenty of water for two and a half to three hours.

# Horse Meat

The horse meat currently eaten in Iceland is mainly from young horses. It's very tender and quite similar to beef. In past days the meat was almost always salted in large barrels and kept for quite some time. It tended to be very tough, though, and had to be boiled for a long time.

# Ram Testicles

When the ram is slaughtered, the scrotum is cut off as a whole. Then the testicles are removed, cleaned, and thoroughly trimmed.

The most common method of preparing them for consumption is to boil them in lightly salted water and, while hot, press them firmly into a flat-bottomed vessel, such as a pan. As they cool they and the liquid pressed out of them form a block of stiff aspic, which is cut into pieces and put in sour whey. The sour testicles are eaten by themselves or, often, with potatoes and Swedish turnips.

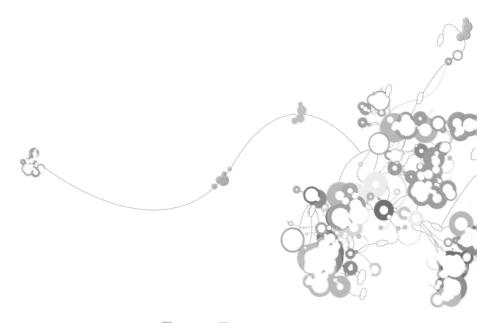

# Lundabaggi

I have always been very fond of food treated in sour whey. One of my favourites is called "lundabaggi" in Icelandic (tenderloin bale) and is, perhaps, an Icelandic specialty.

The large intestine from a sheep is cut open lengthwise and cleaned and scraped most thoroughly. It's then put in salted water for some time, after which it's filled with strips of tenderloin, the heart, the flank, and so on. These should preferably be quite a bit on the fat side. The intestine is wrapped around the filling and tied up tightly, forming a rather stout sausage, and cooked till it is tender.

# OUNCES,
## GRAMS, DECILITERS

| Ounces (dry) | grams |
|---|---|
| 1 oz | 26 g |
| 2 oz | 55 g |
| 3 oz | 85 g |
| 4 oz | 115 g |
| 5 oz | 140 g |
| 6 oz | 170 g |
| 7 oz | 200 g |
| 8 oz | 225 g |
| 9 oz | 250 g |
| 10 oz | 285 g |
| 15 oz | 430 g |
| 20 oz | 570 g |
| 30 oz | 860 g |
| 35 oz | 1 kg |

| Ounces (fluid) | deciliters |
|---|---|
| 1 oz | ¼ dl |
| 2 oz | ½ dl |
| 3 oz | 1 dl |
| 4 oz | 1 ¼ dl |
| 5 oz | 1 ½ dl |
| 6 oz | 1 ¾ dl |
| 7 oz | 2 dl |
| 8 oz | 2 ¼ dl |
| 9 oz | 2 ½ dl |
| 10 oz | 3 dl |
| 15 oz | 4 ¼ dl |
| 20 oz | 6 dl |
| 30 oz | 9 dl |
| 35 oz | 1 l |

## Aïoli

1 large egg
3 tablespoons cider vinegar
½ teaspoon salt
1 teaspoon Dijon mustard
1¼ cups oil (vegetable, olive, and/or canola)
4-6 cloves garlic, minced fine
1 teaspoon lemon juice

Put the egg, vinegar, salt and mustard, along with two tablespoons of oil, in a blender and mix them for a few seconds. While the blender is still running, pour in the remaining oil and stop the blender immediately when the oil is mixed in. Now, by hand, stir in the garlic and the lemon juice. Refrigerate the aïoli.

## Beans, Cooking Them

Begin by spreading the beans out on a kitchen towel. Inspect them closely and discard any broken or shriveled ones. Next, wash the beans thoroughly.

Most beans need to be soaked before they are cooked. If this is the case with the variety in question, put the beans in a bowl, measuring the volume, and add three times more water. The soaking time can vary between types of beans, but usually it is about six hours.

When the soaking is through, drain the water off the beans and put them in a pot with fresh water. The water should be about one and a half times the volume of the soaked beans. Now bring the beans to a boil and then lower the heat to a simmer. Generally, the cooking time for beans is thirty minutes to two hours, depending on the variety in question. The beans can be spiced during the cooking process. If seasoning with

garlic, oregano, parsley or thyme, for example, these can be added to the pot while the beans are cooking. In the case of acid seasonings, such as tomatoes, vinegar, wine or citrus juices, these should only be added toward the end of the cooking time, when the beans have become tender. Salt, on the other hand, should only be added at the very end of the cooking, as, if added earlier, the salt may make the skin on the beans resistant, thus hindering the process of tenderizing.

When done, cool the beans in the cooking liquid to prevent them from becoming dry and shriveled.

## Barbeque Sauce, Spiced

Makes about 1½ cups.
1 tablespoon dried oregano
1 tablespoon paprika
2 cloves garlic, chopped fine
1 teaspoon fresh chili pepper, chopped fine
4 whole fresh cloves
1 whole black peppercorn
2 tablespoons whole mustard seeds
2 star anis
1 teaspoon all spice
1 teaspoon coriander
1 tablespoon fresh ginger, chopped
1 teaspoon cayenne pepper
1 small bay leaf

Put the above dry ingredients in a hot pot and stir well for one minute to bring out the flavor of all the spices.

¾ cup ketchup
2 tablespoons Worcestershire sauce
½ cup water
6 tablespoons red wine vinegar
3 tablespoons Soy sauce
1 tablespoon brown sugar

After having heated the dry ingredients above in the pot, add the vinegar and the soy sauce and bring to a boil. Now add the rest of the ingredients, cover the pot and simmer its contents for one hour. Then strain the mixture and thin it out with water if needed.

## Beef Stock

Yields: about one gallon of stock
8 lb beef bones, including knuckle bones, trimmings, etc., sawn into pieces three to four inches in length.
Oil
6-7 quarts cold water
8 oz onions, coarsely chopped
4 oz carrots, coarsely chopped
4 oz celery, coarsely chopped
8 oz tomatoes, quartered
3 oz tomato paste, thinned with 2 tablespoons water
3 or 4 parsley stems, chopped
½ teaspoon thyme leaves
1 bay leaf
1 whole clove
½ teaspoon cracked black peppercorns
1 clove garlic, crushed

Heat the oven to 400°F/205°C. Then lightly oil a sheet pan and place it in the oven to heat up. When the pan is hot, place the bones on the sheet pan and roast them for thirty minutes, turning them occasionally. After the thirty minutes are up, take the bones out of the oven and brush them with a thin layer of the thinned tomato paste. Then put the bones into the oven again and roast them for 30 minutes more or until they have become evenly brown, turning them occasionally.

Now place the bones in a large pot, cover them with cold water and turn

DELICIOUS ICELAND  148

the heat on. When the water is boiling, lower the heat to simmer. Any froth that is formed on top must be skimmed off. The stock is simmered for six to seven hours.

While the bones are simmering, drain and reserve the fat; deglaze the pan with water, and add it to the pot. If necessary, more hot water can be added to the pot to keep the bones covered.

Toss the onions, carrots and celery with the fat reserved from the oven pan and brown them in the oven. Add these browned ingredients to the tomatoes and the parsley stems, thyme, bay leaves, clove, peppercorns and garlic. Mix all these ingredients slightly and place them on a four inch square piece of cheesecloth and tie the cloth into a sack. Put the sack in the pot with the bones and simmer for one to two hours more.

When this extra simmering is through, strain the stock through a china cap lined with cheesecloth into a container and cool the stock liquid container in an ice-water bath. Finally, transfer the stock to a fitting vessel and refrigerate overnight. The next day, skim off all the fat that has risen to the surface.

## Beet Juice Reduction

4 cups fresh or bottled beet juice
1 cup red wine
2 sprigs fresh rosemary
1 teaspoon demiglaze (See appendix)
1 cup water

Put the beet juice and the red wine in a large sauce pan and bring the mixture to a boil on medium heat. Then simmer until the mixture has been reduced to half its original volume.

Now whisk the demiglaze stock into the reduction and add the sprigs of rosemary. Again, reduce the mixture until the reduction coats the back of a spoon, but not too thickly, though. When done, the reduction should be dark-Burgundy in color. Finally, strain the mixture through a rather fine-meshed sieve, put the liquid in a container and put a lid on it.

## Beet Root Sauce

32 oz. quality beet root Juice
2 tablespoon demiglaze
(See appendix)
Salt and pepper

Reduce beet root juice down by half on medium heat in a sauce pan, stir in two tablespoons of demiglaze. Season to taste with salt and pepper.

## Beurre Blanc Sauce

2 tablespoons shallots, finely chopped
8 oz white wine
2 oz fresh lemon juice
4 tablespoons heavy cream
14 tablespoons cold unsalted butter, cut in cubes
Salt and white pepper

Begin by chopping the shallots and then sautéing them in a saucepan. Add the white wine and the lemon juice and put the heat on high. Reduce the mixture until its volume is about two tablespoons.

Add the cream to the reduction. Once the liquid starts to bubble, turn the heat down. Cut the butter in cubes and add them in one cube at a time, whisking and keeping the saucepan on the heat in the beginning and then

removing it. Keep whisking the butter into the reduction until all the butter is melted and the mixture is fully emulsified and has reached the consistency of a rich sauce. Season the sauce to taste with salt and pepper.

Note: Care must be taken not to boil the sauce after the butter has been added to it. If it boils, the sauce will separate.

## Blanching

Blanching most often refers to fruit and vegetables. The method is to prepare a pot with boiling salted water. Also, a vessel is filled with ice water and placed nearby. The food in question is plunged into the boiling water, left there for only a short time and then removed and cooled instantly in ice water.

Through this treatment, the food in question remains firm and the natural flavor pronounced. This is good preparation for food that is to be frozen. Also, blanching is very useful for preparing food that is to be peeled, such as peaches, plums and tomatoes, as the treatment loosens the skin of the fruit and greatly eases the process of removing the peel.

## Blini

Yield: 16 small pancakes
1 pound white potatoes
2 tablespoons flour
2-3 tablespoons crème fraîche
2 eggs
1 yolk
Vegetable oil for cooking

Peel the potatoes and cook them until they're soft; be careful not to overcook.

Then cut the potatoes into even pieces and mash them . Next, whisk in the flour and crème fraîche. Add first one egg to the mixture and then the other, finally adding the yolk. The finished batter should have the consistency of ordinary pancake batter.

Warm a shallow pan to medium heat and add a splash of vegetable oil. Using a ladle, pour in small pancakes, a little over 2 inches in diameter, and fry them until they're golden brown on both sides.

The pancakes go very well with, for example, smoked salmon or Russian or Iranian caviar.

## Braised Lamb Shanks
4 lamb shanks
Salt and pepper
2 tablespoons olive oil
1 onion, peeled and chopped
1 carrot peeled and chopped
1 stalk celery peeled and chopped
4 cloves garlic, peeled and chopped
1 cup red wine
2 quarts lamb stock (See appendix)

Preheat the oven to 250°F/120°C. Season the shanks with the salt and pepper. Sear the shanks in a large roasting pan over medium high heat until dark brown on all sides. Remove the shanks and set aside. Add the vegetables to the pan and sauté until browned. Deglaze the pan with the red wine and reduce by half. Add the lamb stock and braise the meat for 5-7 hours or until the meat starts to fall off the bone. Remove the lamb shanks and strain the liquid. In a new sauce pot reduce the liquid to approximately 2 cups while skimming the surface for impurities. Before serving warm up the

shanks in the braising liquid and serve with the reduced sauce.

## Broccoli Purée
An 11 oz head of broccoli
4 oz cream cheese
½ teaspoon Nutmeg
Lemon juice
Salt and pepper

First the broccoli florets are either boiled in water or steamed until they have become soft. Then, the broccoli is strained a little and after that put in a food processor along with the nutmeg and cream cheese and puréed until the mixture is completely smooth. The purée is seasoned to taste with the lemon juice and salt and pepper. The purée can be served either hot or cold.

## Brunoise
Brunoise is made using various vegetables, chosen for the specific taste desired. Begin by washing and trimming them thoroughly. Next chop the vegetables into cubes or bits about an eighth of an inch in size and mix them well. The mixture is best used fresh, but it can also be lightly sautéed in butter, for example, if a taste variant is desired.

## Carrot Purée
3 pounds carrots, peeled, cut into half - inch slices
2 tablespoons honey
⅓ cup fresh orange juice
½ cup butter, cut into pieces at room temperature
1 ½ tablespoons minced, peeled fresh ginger
1 tablespoon grated orange peel
1 tablespoon fresh lemon juice

Boil the carrots and 1½ tablespoons of honey in a large pot of salted water.

Stop the cooking when the carrots have become very tender or after about 25 minutes.

Put the carrots in a strainer and drain them well. Then put the carrots into the same pot, empty of water, and stir them over medium heat until any excess moisture has evaporated.

While the carrots are cooking, simmer the orange juice in a small heavy saucepan over medium heat. Add the butter, ginger and orange peel to the orange juice and heat the mixture until the butter melts. Then whisk in the lemon juice and the remaining honey.

Purée half of the carrots and half of the juice mixture in a food processor until the mixture has become a smooth paste. Then transfer the paste to a large bowl, and repeat the procedure with the remaining carrots and juice mixture.

Season the purée to taste with salt and pepper.

The carrot purée can be prepared the day previous to its being used. If this is done, cover the bowl with plastic wrap and put it in a refrigerator. When the purée is to be used, warm it in a microwave oven on high for about four minutes or put the purée in a saucepan over medium to low heat and stir frequently.

## Cassis Sauce
3 cups Crème de Cassis wine
3 tablespoon demiglaze (See appendix)
1 pt water
Fresh thyme

Begin by bringing the water to a boil. Dissolve the demiglaze completely in the water, and then set it aside. Reduce the cassis wine to half its original volume in a medium-sized saucepan. Now add the demiglaze mixture and the thyme to the cassis-wine reduction and bring the blend to a boil at medium heat. Continue boiling until the liquid has thickened so that it lightly coats the back of a spoon.

## Coffee Ice Cream
2 cups heavy cream
2 cups milk
½ cup coffee beans,
8 egg yolks
¾ cup sugar
An ice cream machine

Place the coffee beans in an oven tray and roast them in an oven at 350°F/170°C for fifteen minutes. Stir the beans occasionally during the roasting. Let the beans cool a bit and then grind them very fine in a coffee grinder.

Put the ground coffee beans in a saucepan along with the cream and the milk and bring the blend to a boil.

Remove the saucepan from the heat and let it stand aside for an hour for the beans to infuse their flavor.

Whisk together the egg yolks and sugar in a medium bowl. Pour the cream mixture into the egg yolks, whisking continuously until the ingredients are well-blended. Return this mixture to the saucepan and cook over medium heat, stirring constantly with a flat spatula. Let the spatula reach the bottom, stroking it, to make sure that the saucepan bottom does not heat up too quickly, forming scrapings from the custard as it thickens. When ready, the custard should be thick enough to coat the back of a wooden spoon.

Strain the custard through a fine-mesh sieve and cool the liquid down. Finally, put the mixture in an ice cream machine and freeze it.

## Couscous, how to Cook
1 cup uncooked couscous
1¼ cups water
¼ teaspoon kosher salt
1 teaspoon butter

Begin by putting the water, along with the salt and butter, into a saucepan and bringing it to a boil. When the liquid in the saucepan is boiling, add the couscous and stir briskly.

When all the couscous has been stirred in, take the saucepan off the heat, cover it, and set it aside for four to five minutes. Before the couscous is served, it should be whipped up a little with a fork to make it somewhat fluffy.

## Crème Anglaise
½ pint milk
1 vanilla pod
3 egg yolks, beaten
1 tablespoon caster sugar

Pour the milk into a saucepan. Split the vanilla pod open and scrape the beans out of it. Then put the beans and the pod into the milk and heat it slowly until it is almost boiling. Then remove the saucepan from the heat, and leave the mixture to infuse for about 20 minutes, after which time the vanilla pod is removed.

Next, put the egg yolks and the sugar together in a bowl and stir the blend until it becomes thick and creamy. Then gradually whisk the hot milk in with the egg yolks and sugar.

When the mixing is done, strain the mixture back into the saucepan. Put the saucepan on the stove and cook the liquid over low heat, stirring constantly for ten to twenty minutes or until the custard thickens enough to lightly coat the back of a wooden spoon. Do not allow the custard to boil or it will curdle.

Finally, strain the custard into a bowl and let it cool.

## Demiglaze
Yield: 1 quart
4 oz onions, diced medium
2 oz carrots, diced medium
2 oz celery, diced medium
2 oz butter
2 oz flour
1 ½ quart beef stock (See appendix)
2 oz tomato purée
1 bay leaf
Pinch of thyme
Pinch parsley stems

First sauté the onions, the carrots, and the celery in butter until they are well-browned. Then add the flour and stir to make a roux. Continue cooking until the roux has turned brown. Gradually stir the tomato purée into the roux.

Now add the beef stock, stirring constantly, and let the mixture reduce for about two hours or until the demiglaze thickly covers the back of a spoon. Skim off the froth formed as necessary. When the simmering is done, strain the mixture through a china cap lined with several layers of cheesecloth. Press the cloth gently to extract the juices as far as possible. Put the demiglaze in a metal container and refrigerate.

## Duck Confit

3 tablespoons salt
6 cloves garlic, smashed
1 shallot, peeled and sliced
6 sprigs thyme
4-6 duck legs with thighs
4-6 cups duck fat
Black pepper, coarsely ground

Sprinkle 1 tablespoon of salt in the bottom of a container large enough to hold the duck pieces in a single layer. Evenly scatter half the garlic, shallots, and thyme in the container. Arrange the duck, skin-side up, over the salt mixture, then sprinkle with the remaining salt, garlic, shallots, and thyme and a little pepper. Cover and refrigerate for 1 day.

   Preheat the oven to 225°F/110°C. Melt the duck fat in a saucepan. Brush the salt and seasonings off the duck and arrange the duck pieces in a single, snug layer in a high-sided baking dish. Pour the melted fat over the duck (the duck pieces should be covered by fat) and place the confit in the oven. Cook the confit slowly at a very slow simmer — just an occasional bubble — until the duck is tender and can be easily pulled from the bone, 2-3 hours. Remove the confit from the oven. Cool and store the duck in the fat. (The confit will keep in the refrigerator for two weeks.)

## Edamame Mousse

3 cups heavy cream
2 cups edamame beans
(fresh or frozen)
2 gelatin sheets
½ teaspoon kosher salt
½ teaspoon sugar
2 tablespoons grape seed oil
¼ cup coarsely chopped parsley
½ cup water

Begin by putting six cups of water into a medium-sized pot and bringing it to a boil. Then put the edamame beans, along with the parsley, into the pot, blanch them until the beans are tender (See appendix: blanching), and cool them instantly in ice water. When cold, the beans and the parsley are put in a strainer for the water to drip off and then put aside.

While the beans and the parsley are blanching, put the three cups of heavy cream into a chilled bowl and whisk it until thoroughly whipped and then put it into a refrigerator.

Next, put the strained beans and parsley, along with the salt, the sugar and half of the cup of water in a high-speed food processor and mix the ingredients at top speed until they're thoroughly blended and smooth; at which time, little by little, pour in the oil and mix it in. When done, put the mixture aside.

Put the sheets of gelatin in a bowl of ice water to soften them. When the gelatin has become soft, drain it and put the remainder of the half cup of water in a small saucepan, along with the softened gelatin, and heat until the gelatin has been completely dissolved.

Now take the whipped cream from the refrigerator. Using a rubber spatula mix the bean mixture with the dissolved gelatin and then gently fold in the whipped cream. Great care must be taken not to over-fold, because if done, the mixture will separate. When done with the folding, the mousse is put into a refrigerator to cool and set.

## Fish Stock

1 teaspoon grape seed oil
3 pounds fish bones
1 large carrot
1 onion
2 celery sticks
2 bay leaves
1 teaspoon peppercorn
Juice from one lemon
10 cups water
2 cups dry white wine

Heat a large casserole. Sauté the chopped vegetables and the chopped fish bones in the grape seed oil. Add the wine, water and lemon juice. Simmer uncovered for twenty-five minutes, skimming off any froth as it forms. Finally, strain the stock through a fine sieve lined with cheese-cloth and let it cool down.

## Grapefruit Vinaigrette

Juice from one pink grapefruit
4.3 oz grape seed oil
Salt and Pepper

Put the grapefruit juice and the grape seed oil in a bowl and whisk them together. Then, still whisking, season the mixture to taste with salt and pepper.

## Horseradish Cream

1 cup cream cheese
1 cup whipped cream
2 tablespoons fresh ground horseradish
Juice from one lime
Salt and pepper

Allow the cream cheese to warm up at room temperature and soften. Then gently stir in the horseradish and the lime juice. Add the whipped cream, folding it gently into the mixture, and season to taste with salt and pepper. When finished, the horseradish cream is put in a refrigerator to cool.

## Lamb Stock

Yield: 2 quarts
5 pounds lamb shanks or neck bones
2 medium onions, quartered
2 medium carrots, halved lengthwise
2 bay leaves
4 cloves garlic
2 sprigs thyme
2 sprigs parsley
10 whole black peppercorns
Water

Preheat the oven to 500°F/260°C. Place the lamb shanks or neck bones in a roasting pan and roast them for about 20 minutes or until they have been browned on all sides. While in the oven, the bones should be turned occasionally.

When the roasting is done, transfer the lamb bones to a large stock pot, and add the onions, carrots, bay leaves, thyme, parsley and peppercorns.

Add 1 quart of water to the roasting pan. Heat the water and scrape loose any bits sticking to the bottom of the pan. Pour the liquid from the pan into the stock pot and add 3 quarts of water to cover the bones. Bring the liquid in the pot to a boil and then simmer for 2 hours, skimming occasionally. When the cooking time is up, strain the stock into a large saucepan and let cool. Remove the fat from the top of the lamb stock before using.

## Lemon oil

Zest from ½ lemon
1 ¼ oz grape seed oil
Salt and pepper

Put the lemon zest in 1 cup grape seed oil over very low heat in a small sauce pan for twenty minutes. Put in a blender and blend for 30 seconds. Season with salt and pepper and allow to cool. Strain through a fine sieve before using.

## Lemon scented potato purée

1.5 lbs potatoes
2 cloves garlic, halved, germ removed
3 tablespoons unsalted butter, cut into small pieces
½ - 1 cup cream
Coarse sea salt and freshly ground pepper
Juice of one lemon

Peel and cut the potatoes into 1-inch chunks. Put the potatoes and garlic in a large saucepan and cover with cold water. Add a tablespoon of coarse sea salt.

Place over med-high heat and bring to a boil until soft.

Drain the potatoes and garlic then pass them though a fine sieve, and return to the dry saucepan. Little by little, incorporate the butter, cream and juice of one lemon, mixing with a large spoon. Season to taste with salt and pepper.

## Lemon Vinaigrette

Yield: 1 cup
¼ cup fresh lemon juice
¾ cup grape seed oil
Salt and pepper

Put the lemon juice into a bowl. Slowly whisk in the grape seed oil and season to taste with salt and pepper.

The vinaigrette may be made three hours before it is used. If this is done, it should be covered and chilled. Before use, the vinaigrette may be brought to room temperature.

## Lentil Beans, Cooking Them

1 cup lentil beans
1 ½ cups vegetable stock
(See appendix)

Examine the lentil beans before cook-ing by spreading them out on a white kitchen towel so that any dirt, debris, or damaged specimens can be easily seen and discarded. Then place the remaining lentil beans in a strainer and rinse them well under cold, running water.

After rinsing, the beans are cooked in the vegetable stock, and left to simmer for about fifteen minutes or until they are tender. Add more stock during the cooking, if needed. Finally, strain any excess liquid off the beans.

## Mango Sauce

2 ripe mangoes
2 tablespoons powdered sugar
2 tablespoons mango liqueur
Juice from one fresh lime or lemon

Begin by peeling the mango. Remove the mango flesh, cut it into chunks, and blend them thoroughly in a food processor. Now add the sugar and the mango liqueur and blend on until the mixture is smooth, adding the lime or lemon juice to taste.

Strain the sauce through a fine sieve. Simmer it slowly in a saucepan for five minutes, then allow the sauce to cool.

## Mushroom Stock

1 teaspoon grape seed oil
1 pound wild mushrooms or button mushrooms
3 cloves garlic, chopped
½ onion, chopped
1 sprig thyme
1 bay leaf
3 stalks parsley
½ cup dry sherry
½ cup brandy
8 cups water or vegetable stock
(See appendix)

Begin by cutting the mushrooms into thin slices and sautéing them in the oil in a hot casserole until they start to dry. Next, add the chopped garlic, onion, thyme, bay leaf and parsley and stir for one minute. After this, pour in the sherry and brandy, let them reduce, and then add water or vegetable stock. Now bring the stock to a boil and let it simmer for thirty minutes, skimming off any froth as it forms. Finally, strain the stock through a fine sieve lined with cheesecloth and let it cool down.

## Orange and Mint Syrup

2 tablespoons honey
½ cup fresh orange juice
Juice from one lemon
Segments from one orange, diced
A pinch of fresh mint leaves, finely diced.

First bring the honey, the orange juice and the lemon juice to a boil in a saucepan until the mixture starts to turn syrupy. Then fold in the orange segments and let the contents in the saucepan cool. When the syrup has cooled, put the diced mint leaves into the syrup and serve.

## Orange Reduction

Makes about ¼ cup
1 ¼ cups freshly squeezed orange juice
1 star anis
1 clove garlic, cut in half

Place a pan on the stove and put the ingredients in it. Turn the heat on low and reduce the contents of the pan slowly until it turns thick and syrupy. Finally, strain the liquid through a fine sieve and let it cool.

The orange reduction should be served at room temperature.

## Pasta Dough

8.8 oz plain flour
¼ tablespoon salt
¼ tablespoon olive oil
2 eggs
3 egg yolks

Begin by putting the flour, salt and olive oil in a blender and processing these ingredients for a few seconds. Next, add the eggs and the extra yolks into the blender and process until the pasta begins to come together and form a loose ball of dough.

At this time empty the pasta dough onto a flat surface and knead it well until it has become even and smooth. Then cut the dough into eight equal pieces and roll them into balls. Wrap each ball tightly in a piece of plastic wrap and allow to rest in the refrigerator for twenty minutes. (This is necessary, as no pasta dough can be used immediately). The dough can be frozen for later use.

## Peach Chutney

4 cups firm, ripe, chopped peaches
½ cup vinegar
¼ cup fresh lemon juice
1 cup seedless golden raisins
1 tablespoon finely chopped ginger
⅓ cup finely chopped onion
1 tablespoon salt
1 teaspoon ground allspice
½ teaspoon ground cinnamon
½ teaspoon ground cloves
½ teaspoon ground ginger
½ cup white sugar
¾ cup light brown sugar
1 tablespoon grape seed oil

Begin by sautéing the onion and the ginger for one minute in a large saucepan. Then add all the ingredients except the white and brown sugar. Bring the mixture to a full boil and boil it for five minutes, stirring continuously.

When the time is up, add the white and brown sugar and bring the mixture back to a boil. Boil for two to three minutes more.
   Remove the saucepan from the heat; skim off any froth, and let the chutney cool for ten minutes.

## Pearl Onion Confit

1 cup olive oil or duck fat
¾ cup pearl onions, peeled
1 teaspoon sugar

Heat the olive oil or the duck fat with sugar to 200°F/90°C in a sauce pan. Add the onion and cook gently until soft.

## Pickled Red Onions

2 medium-sized red onions
1 cup red wine vinegar
½ cup water
½ cup sugar
½ teaspoon kosher salt
1 teaspoon black peppercorns
2 star anis
½ tablespoon grape seed oil

Peel the onions and cut them into wedges. Put the grape seed oil into a hot pan and sauté the onions for a minute or two. Put all the other ingredients into the pan on top of the onions and bring to a boil. Cover the pan with a lid or a sheet of aluminum foil, take it off the heat and leave it to cool to room temperature. Finally, put the pickled onions along with the liquid in a container and close it tightly.

## Pickling Liquid

2 cups rice wine vinegar
1 teaspoon black pepper corns
1 teaspoon mustard seeds
1 star anis
4 cloves
1 teaspoon all spice
4 tablespoons sugar

Mix all the ingredients together and bring them to a boil. Allow the mixture to cool and then strain it.

## Port Wine Sauce

1 tablespoon grape seed oil
1 clove garlic, minced
1 shallot, minced
2 cups port wine
2 tablespoons demiglaze
(See appendix)
Small sprig of fresh thyme
Salt and pepper

Sauté the garlic and shallot in a sauce pan with the grape seed oil over medium heat until golden. Then add the port wine and reduce by half on low heat. Stir in the demiglaze and add the sprig of thyme, to infuse, and let simmer for 3 minutes. Season to taste with salt and pepper and strain through a sieve.

## Portobello Mushroom Risotto

1 cup risotto rice
1 tablespoon olive oil
1 large onion, chopped
¼ cup Parmesan cheese, grated
4-5 cups hot mushroom stock
(See appendix)
½ cup white wine
½ cup sautéed diced Portobello mushrooms
Salt and Pepper

Begin by heating the olive oil in a cas-

serole dish and adding the onions, sautéing them in the oil until they are translucent.

Now add the rice and stir until the grains are completely coated with oil, and then add the wine, stirring constantly at medium heat until the wine is absorbed. Next, add one cup of hot mushroom stock and stir until the liquid is absorbed. Continue cooking for about twenty minutes, adding the remaining stock one cup at a time.

The rice creates its own creamy sauce, which can be made creamier, if desired, by adding more stock.

When done, remove the pot from the heat, stir in the cheese and the sautéed Portobello mushrooms. Season to taste with salt and pepper and let cool slightly before use.

## Rabbit Leg Confit

1 lb rabbit legs
2 lb duck fat
1 stalk of thyme, left whole
2 pieces star anise
2 pieces bay leaf
1 stalk of lemongrass, coarsely chopped
1 onion, peeled and coarsely chopped
2 cloves of garlic, peeled and coarsely chopped
Salt and pepper

Begin by melting the duck fat over medium heat. When it has liquefied, add the onion, garlic, lemongrass, bay leaves, star anise, and thyme and reduce the heat to low.

Now season the rabbit legs generously with salt and pepper and put them in the duck fat. Slowly cook the rabbit legs at low heat for approximately two

to three hours, or until the meat is falling off the bone. At this stage turn off the heat and let the rabbit bones cool in the fat. When the fat is cool, remove the legs from the fat, pull the meat off the bone and shred it into strands.

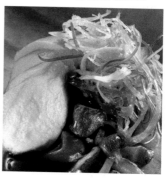

## Red Wine Reduction

1 medium onion coarsely chopped
1 medium bell pepper coarsely chopped
Half a bunch of fresh thyme
1 bottle red wine (750ml)
3 tablespoons demiglaze
(See appendix)
1 teaspoon vegetable oil

Put the vegetable oil in a medium hot pan and add the onions, bell peppers and thyme. Sauté these ingredients until the onions turn golden.

Now turn the heat to high, add the red wine and reduce the mixture by half. At this time, add the demiglaze, lower the heat to medium, and reduce the contents to half the volume.

While reducing, take care to stir frequently to ensure no burning or sticking. The reduction should lightly coat the back of spoon and be dark burgundy in color.

1 teaspoon vegetable oil
2 cups water
A pinch of kosher salt

Put a medium-sized sauté pan on medium heat. Add the oil to the pan and sauté the scallions until they are soft. Then add the wine and reduce the mixture by half. When this has been accomplished, add the sugar, the salt and the water, and cook the marmalade at low heat until all the liquid has been reduced.

The sugar tends to caramelize quickly during this last stage, so be careful not to let the marmalade get brown. Also, stir the marmalade occasionally to keep it from sticking to the pan.

### Sesame Seed Sauce
1 cup honey
Juice from one lemon
¼ cup black and white sesame seeds
Salt and pepper

Begin by toasting the sesame seeds in a pan until the white seeds are golden in color. Then add the honey and remove from the heat, mixing in the lemon juice and seasoning with salt and pepper to taste. Place the sauce in a container and allow it cool.

### Sherry Vinaigrette
1 teaspoon Dijon mustard
2 teaspoons finely chopped shallots
1 tablespoon sherry wine vinegar
3 tablespoons olive oil

Mix together the mustard, shallots and vinegar. When perfectly blended, whisk in the olive oil.

### Spicy Ratatouille
1 eggplant, diced into ½-inch chunks
1 green bell pepper, cut into ½-inch squares

### Raspberry Sauce
10 oz. fresh raspberries
Sugar, to taste
1 teaspoon cornstarch
1 teaspoon cold water

Put raspberries in a food processor for 30 seconds, add sugar to taste, and strain into a small saucepan. Bring to a simmer. Dissolve the cornstarch in the water, then add it to the sauce a little bit at a time to thicken it and let simmer for 4 minutes. Strain through a sieve and cool.

### Sauvignon Blanc Froth
½ quart Sauvignon Blanc
4 tablespoons cold butter
Salt and pepper

Reduce the wine by half. Add the cold butter and blend with a hand blender. Season with salt and pepper.

### Scallion Marmalade
3 cups finely chopped scallions
1 cup dry white wine
1 teaspoon sugar

1 red bell pepper, cut into ½-inch squares
3 zucchini, sliced ½-inch thick
4 tomatoes cut in 1-inch chunks
1 large onion, chopped
1 red chili pepper, chopped
2 cloves garlic, minced
¼ cup dry white wine
½ lemon
¼ cup olive oil
1 bunch fresh thyme, secured with string
¼ cup fresh basil, chopped
2 bay leaves
1 teaspoon salt
1 teaspoon black pepper

Begin by heating the olive oil in a large pot and then sautéing the chopped onion until it becomes translucent. Next add the garlic, the thyme bunch, the basil, salt and pepper, and the bay leaves. Cook these ingredients for about two minutes. Then add the tomatoes and the wine. Simmer the mixture for thirty minutes without a cover on the pot, stirring occasionally.

When the thirty minutes of simmering are up, add the eggplant, the zucchini and the red and green peppers, and continue simmering for about fifteen minutes, or until the vegetables have become tender, stirring gently now and then and taking care not to break up the vegetables.

The ratatouille is best, if allowed to chill overnight in a refrigerator. It can be served cold, warm or hot. Remember to remove the bunch of thyme before the ratatouille is served.

### Thyme and Orange Brine
1 quart boiling water
¼ cup kosher salt

½ bunch fresh thyme
1 garlic cloves, peeled and halved
1 tablespoon coarsely cracked
peppercorns
1 orange, halved
4 tablespoon sugar

Combine the boiling water, salt, thyme, garlic, orange and sugar. Bring the mixture to a boil and make sure all the sugar has dissolved. Then strain the brine and let it cool.

### Tomato Risotto
1 cup Risotto rice
1 tablespoon olive oil
1 large onion, chopped
¼ cup Parmesan cheese, grated
4-5 cups hot vegetable stock
(See appendix)
½ cup white wine
½ cup sautéed diced tomatoes
½ cup sautéed diced scallions

First heat the olive oil in a casserole and then sauté the onions in the oil until they are translucent. Now add the rice and stir it until the grains are completely coated with oil. Then add the wine, stirring constantly at medium heat until the wine is absorbed. Next, add one cup of hot vegetable stock or water and stir until the liquid is absorbed. The cooking is continued for about twenty minutes and the remaining liquid added one cup at a time. The rice creates its own creamy sauce, which can be made creamier, if desired, by adding more liquid.

For variety, fresh herbs and chopped vegetables can be added during the last five minutes of cooking. When done, remove the pot from the heat, stir in the cheese and serve the risotto hot.

### Vegetable Stock
1 teaspoon grape seed oil
4 large carrots
2 stalks of leek
3 celery stalks
½ bulb of fennel
2 onions
1 parsnip
2 cloves garlic
3 stalks parsley,
1 sprig thyme
1 bay leaf,
1 teaspoon grape seed oil
2 cups dry white wine
10 cups water
1 teaspoon white peppercorns
Juice from one lemon

All the vegetables must be washed and drained thoroughly and all the root vegetables peeled. When this is done, chop all the vegetables into very small pieces. Put all the vegetables in a hot casserole with the oil and stir until golden brown. Then add the wine and the water and all the other ingredients. Now bring the mixture to a boil and let it simmer for thirty minutes. Skim any froth off as it forms. Finally, strain the stock through a fine sieve lined with cheesecloth and let it cool down.

### Walnut Vinaigrette
5 oz brown sugar
3 oz Westchester sauce
½ cup (4oz) Dijon mustard
12 fl. oz walnut oil
4.5 oz- red wine vinegar

Put all the above ingredients in a bowl and mix them together thoroughly.

### Wasabi Oil
8 oz grape seed oil
1 cup wasabi powder
Salt
¼ cup water

Put the wasabi powder in a medium sized bowl and stir in water until a soft ball is formed. Leave it uncovered for about five minutes.

Next, crumble the ball of wasabi into a medium-sized saucepan and add the oil and a pinch of salt. Now work the crumbled wasabi and the oil into a loose paste and then put the saucepan on the stove at medium heat until all the water has evaporated. Take care to stir constantly so that the wasabi does not burn. The oil is ready when it is clear and has separated from the wasabi.

When the oil and the wasabi have become separated in the pot, strain the mixture through a fine strainer, such as a coffee filter. The oil dripping down should be completely clear, free of any water and light green in color.